Marina Baker's

# Teenage

## survival guide

**M**arina Baker is a journalist, author, witch and environmental campaigner. Her first book, *Spells for Teenage Witches*, published in autumn 2000, reprinted within a week of publication and has reprinted regularly ever since. *Spells for Teenage Witches* and Marina's second book, *Spells for the Witch in You*, have now sold over 150,000 copies worldwide. *Teenage Survival Guide* was inspired by the many letters and emails she has received from readers of the first two books.

Marina Baker is married with two small children and a beautiful teenage step-daughter. She lives in Brighton.

# Marina Baker's

# Teenage survival guide

Whitecap

This edition published in Canada by Whitecap Books
351 Lynn Avenue, North Vancouver, BC, Canada V7J 2C4
www.whitecap.ca

First published in 2002 by Kyle Cathie Limited

ISBN 1 55285 378 0

This book is printed on paper from a sustainable source

Edited by Caroline Taggart
Designed by Mark Buckingham and Geoff Hayes
Production by Lorraine Baird and Sha Huxtable
See illustration acknowledgements on page 8

Marina Baker is hereby identified as the author of this
work in accordance with Section 77 of the Copyright,
Designs and Patents Act 1988.

A Cataloguing in Publication record for this title is available
from the British Library.

Printed in Spain by Artes Gráficas Toledo SA,
Mondadori Group

We do not inherit the world from our ancestors
We are loaned it by our children

This book is dedicated to the memory of Michael Hallaghan, born 11 September 1952, passed through the veil 3 December 2001. You live on in our hearts and the flowers in our gardens.

# Acknowledgements

*Thank you to:*
Peps for cooking, cleaning and holding the kids

Charlie and Boudicca for letting mummy work

Rosie, my darling step-daughter, for keeping me abreast of all things teenage. Plus, welcoming me and the kids into your and daddy's life. With love

Abby for your pictures and not having a car but still recycling

Nancy for trawling the web in the quest for knowledge (hope you took regular screen breaks)

Jojo for your contribution to the drop-in coven and the quest. Thank you for coming to Avebury at the drop of a besom

Ed for discussing deities

Justine for listening

The staff and volunteers at Martletts Hospice, Brighton, for your dedicated care of Mickey and us, his extended family

The Saltdean Mothers for everything

Ade and Billy for your party spirits

Julia for realizing there was a book here somewhere

Kyle for listening to Julia

Caroline for finding the book in here somewhere

Geoff and Mark for coping

King Arthur Uther Pendragon for your dedication to the cause

Pete Jennings. Was Hail! and ta for the book

Clive "I'm not depressed, I'm an environmental scientist" Pepe and all at riverOcean. Big love for the blinding observation: we all live downstream

And a big wordup to all the charities, pressure groups, volunteers and followers of all spiritual paths who work tirelessly to make the world a better place for all

Merry Meet My Friends

# Picture acknowledgements

**Key**: AH = Abby Hughes; MB = Mark Buckingham; GH = Geoff Hayes; Still = Still Pictures; SPL = Science Photo Library; GPL = Garden Picture Library; Holt = Holt Studios International; JP = Juliet Piddington

page 2 AH; 4 MB; 10, 12, 16 AH; 15 Still/NASA; 19, 20 AH; 21 & 35 Still/B & C Alexander; 24, 27 AH; 29 Holt/Primrose Peacock; 28 MB; 31, 32, 36 AH; 39 Holt/Nigel Cattlin; 40, 41 AH; 42 Still/Mark Edwards; 45 AH; 47 SPL/Alfred Pasteka; 48 GPL/Dennis Davis; 52 Still/J J Alcalay; 55 AH; 56 Still/François Gilson; 59 GPL/Jiri Merz; 60 Holt/Nigel Cattlin; 61 JP; 62 MB; 63 GPL/Vaughan Fleming; 65, 66/7, 68, 71, 72, 74 AH; 76/7 Holt/Nigel Cattlin; 78 GPL/Clive Nichols; 79 Holt/Nigel Cattlin; 81, 83, 84/5 AH; 86 Still/J P Delobelle; 87 MB; 89 AH; 91 Still/Patrick Bertrand; 93 Still/Frederic Denhez; 94, 97, 98 AH; 101 MB; 103, 104 AH; 107, 108 MB; 110 JP; 111 Still/Peter Weimann; 112 Still/Werner H Muller; 114 AH; 114/115 Still/William Fautre; 119 Clive Druett/Corbis; 121, 122/3, 125, 126/7 AH; 130 JP; 131 AH; 132 MB; 133, 134/5 AH; 138 SPL/Science Pictures Ltd; 139 SPL/Pascal Goetgheluck; 140 MB; 143, 144, 149, 150/1, 155, 156 AH; 153 Gus Filgate; 159 GH; 161 AH; 162/3 GH; 164/5 Still/Brill-Line; 166/7, 168 AH; 170/1 MB; 172 Still/Clyde H. Smith; 174/5 JP; 176 Gary Halsall; 177 AH; 179 MB; 180 AH; 183 GPL/A I Lord; 184 GPL/Kit Young; 187 AH; 189 GH; 191 AH; 192 GH; 195, 197 AH; 201 MB; 203 AH; 205 GH; 206, 209, 211 MB; 213 Still/UNEP; 214 GH; 217 MB; 218 Still/Tomas D Mangelsen; 229, 233 AH.

# Contents

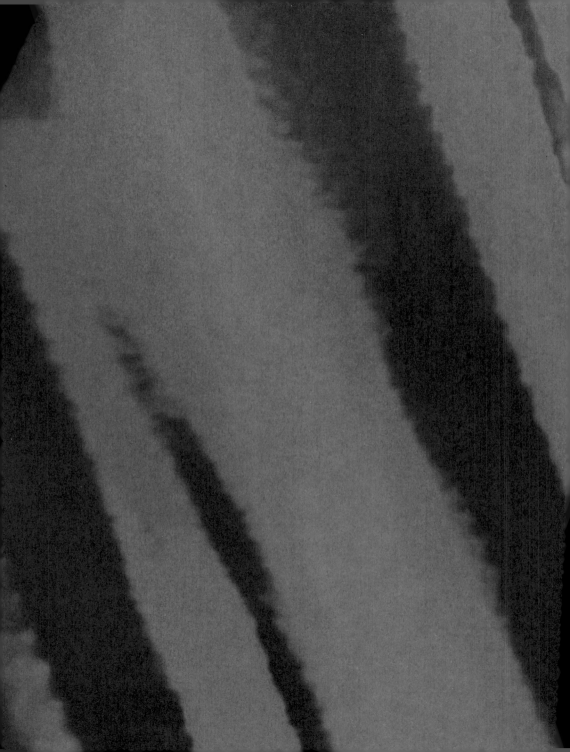

# Introduction

The way I see it, we're all teenagers really. The whole of humanity. Learning to accept responsibility for our actions, which is what being a grown-up is all about. Understanding that what we do can harm ourselves and others. Realizing we can do positive things to make a difference, too. It's all perfectly straightforward.

To be honest, though, between you and me, I don't think humanity's taking adolescence very well. If we've been told once, we've been told a thousand times, "You're only hurting yourselves." Hurting how? Through pollution, global warming, rising sea levels, mass extinction of mammals, plants and other life forms… Do I need to go on? You'd think not.

Yet how has humanity responded? It has stomped off to its bedroom to sulk. Like if we ignore the issues for long enough, they will go away. Very childish.

And bloody typical. There's you trying to cope with genuine teenage problems, like exams, hormonal rushes, spots, the nuances of dating and a school bully who really is upsetting people. On top of all that you're now expected to save the world (and do your homework on time). Why? Because, as grown-ups are very fond of saying, "No one's going to do it for you."

Why can't adults just pull themselves together and grow up? Maybe they will, eventually, if we set them a good enough example.

This is going to be much more fun than you might imagine. Just join the growing band of merry thinkers of all ages and from all walks of life, creating the revolution known as the (no)alternative movement. (No)alternatives are merry because this is no time to get depressed. Our motto: be a good ancestor. Our

mission: to save the world. The plan: well, the plan's rather up to you. Either you choose to be part of the problem or you choose to be the solution. It's not a case of denying ourselves. It's about cherishing the gifts of life and preserving them for future generations. A joyous experience, surely.

As Mahatma Gandhi once said, "We must be the change we wish to see in the world." And as a great modern Druid, King Arthur Uther Pendragon, puts it, "How do we save the world? Do what we can, where we can, when we can."

Join the (no)alternatives and health, love, peace and happiness will be ours. What more could we possibly want?

Blessed Be.

Marina

xxx

P S: I'm a witch, by the way. Not all (no)alternatives are witches. But witches do tend to be (no)alternatives. We're magical, but we live in the real world. The very real world. I would say it's a jungle out there. But there's not much jungle left. It's more like a crazy-paving concrete patio from horizon to horizon.

Now what we need to do is get you through the traumas of the teen years with as little stress as possible. Then you can take your place in the grown-up world and sort it out. This book is crammed with tips and spells to help you do just that.

P P S: Don't worry about all those sulking adults. They'll come downstairs eventually. Let's hope there's still some dinner left when they do.

A spell is a blend of prayer, promise and intent. When you cast a spell you acknowledge yourself as the true author of your destiny. Some spells exert influence on others. If we suspect a spell might cause harm, we resist the urge to cast it. This in itself often requires a spell.

A well-cast spell brings positive change or maintains what is good. The success of all spells depends on our determination to make the "wish" come true.

# Prepare for a spell

# The Wiccan Rede

*THROUGHOUT THIS BOOK THERE ARE QUOTATIONS TAKEN FROM THE WICCAN REDE, WHICH IS A KIND OF RULE OF THUMB FOR WITCHES. THIS POEM IS ALLEGEDLY ANCIENT BUT WAS NEVER PUBLISHED — PUBLICLY AT LEAST — UNTIL THE 1970S. IT OFFERS SOME SOUND ADVICE ABOUT ALLOWING LOVE TO GUIDE US IN ALL WE DO, TO CARE FOR OUR WORLD AND FOR OTHERS.*

The best known lines include, "Mind the Threefold law ye should, three times bad and three times good." And: "Eight words the wiccan rede fulfil, An ye harm none, do what ye will."

The first couplet means that whatever you are doing, be it a spell or a shopping trip, how you behave, think and feel will influence your "luck". A hurtful spell will cause you great harm – just you wait and see. If you are rude or dishonest, retribution will come. And it will be three times worse than your intent towards others.

The second couplet means if your activities are harmless, get on with it. This is a very useful line of argument with parents when they nag you to be more like them and really, you'd rather not. Just ask, "Who am I harming?" Obviously if you're causing your parents untold stress, then that's harmful. But if you're simply pointing out that they should turn the lights off when they leave a room, then continue – just don't nag. They hate to be nagged as much as you do. See the Glossary on page 228 to find out more about the *Wiccan Rede*, a highly influential poem

that inspired all witches and pagans to become (no)alternatives – because there is no alternative.

## A witch's Tools

Witches are quite theatrical. We could cast spells using just our hands and our minds. But we like props. That's why our cupboards are always crammed with ingredients so we're not caught short when a spell's needed. Well, you never know who's going to come to the door, asking for help, do you?

In spells we may use some or all of the following: incense, essential oils, feathers, crystals, stones, driftwood, ribbons, threads, needles, candles, tapers, candle holders, silk cloth, cotton cloth, herbs, cups and flowers (dried, fresh and potted).

In addition a witch will have an altar, a wand, pentacles (if you don't know what they are, see page 163), a besom (broomstick), a lunar calendar plus a selection of gardening tools for the herb, flower, vegetable and wildlife gardens.

What makes these things magical is the intent and the circumstances in which they are used. We bring about positive change through casting a spell and having the determination to ensure our "wish" comes true.

But don't worry about having all the ingredients to hand immediately. You have to live the magic, live the life first. Be a witch. Witches are helpful, kind and loving. We revere the Elements: Air, Water, Earth and Fire – these are the natural materials that make up our world. We also revere Spirit, life, the non-material that is very real all the same.

Understand the importance of the Elements and Spirit. Whatever adults think, we dance to the Elements' tune. It is not the other way around. Know this and you will be a witch and your spells will take care of themselves.

## Note to self

Any item that could be potentially dangerous in the wrong hands, be it innocent children or ignorant adults, will be kept firmly under lock and key or hidden well out of the way.

The rest of this chapter is dedicated to the most essential items for the witch. There are others detailed in the glossary on page 228.

## Essential life Tool 1 ✪
## Lunar calendar

If we follow the cycles of the moon, from new to full and round again, it has a profound effect on our attitude to everything natural in the world and to life. It is as though the Goddess utters a plea. She asks us to engage emotionally with our surroundings. Once we do this, it is impossible to turn away. That is how love is created and sustained. That's how the moon speaks to me.

She might have a personal message for you. So don't forget to look up into the star-lit skies from time to time.

To give thanks for her inspiration, each month when the moon is full witches celebrate with an esbat (the witchy name for a witchy gathering on a full moon). Sometimes spells are cast – magical powers are said to increase threefold at this time. Sometimes we scry (look into the future or deep within ourselves – they appear to be one and the same thing).

Whatever occurs it is most definitely a Spiritual time, a moment to take stock, a breather from the harsh realities of modern living. We accept that the moon was there before and the moon will still be there long after we are gone. It can be quite an awe-inspiring thought.

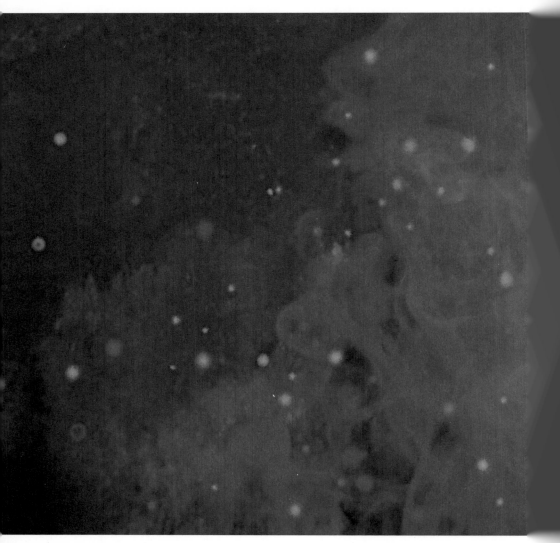

The days following a full moon, when she is waning, are seen as a good time to give up those habits we'd rather not have. When the moon is new, we like to take on positive changes. This is the time of the waxing moon.

It also provides an excellent couple of weeks for planting seeds. They draw in more water at this time. They grow more quickly and strongly. Honestly – it's been scientifically proven. It means you can get them potted up faster and make more room on the window-sills for planting as the next full moon approaches. If you garden. And witches and (no)alternatives do.

The full moon is also a time for love, so watch you don't get moonstruck. It really does happen. Believe me.

Our coven wouldn't be without our lunar calendar, which tells us the precise time of the full and the new moons. Nor should you. Contact riverOcean (details on page 236) to get one. If nothing else, it will remind you to look up. And once you look, once you've seen her and acknowledged her presence, you'll find her plea impossible to resist.

# Moonbathing

Either outside or in your bedroom, expose your skin – all of it – to the light of the moon. Experiment with different phases of her cycle. You may find that you can feel the difference between a full and a quarter moon. Try it.

# Gods and Goddesses

Many of the old gods, sacred to our ancestors since the dawn of time, have been sleeping. Without the bustle and theatrics of ritual worship they nodded off. They couldn't die, because they were never totally forgotten. They lived through our folklore and superstitions. We invoke their protection still whenever we throw spilled salt over our shoulder, grow bay trees outside our homes or touch wood.

But not all of them have been snoozing. Some have spent the last 2000 years happily disguised as saints, keeping a hand in, living exemplary lives, helping and inspiring the faithful. Brigit is one of the great long-lived survivors. She began her career in primeval times as a fire Goddess. She went on to herald spring in Scotland and aid healers, poets and blacksmiths in Ireland. She later attended the birth of Christ as his midwife and, five centuries on, opened the first nunnery in Ireland. She is now number two patron saint of Ireland after St Patrick and is also the saint of journalists in the UK, who have a church dedicated to her. What a girl!

Other deities worshipped by the Hindus or the indigenous peoples of Australia, America and Tibet, among others, have remained wide awake and of practical use to their followers.

Now the sleeping gods the world over are stirring, ready to join them. I sense them rolling over, having a stretch, a yawn and a good old scratch. As they focus their eyes, they look around in dismay. "What's been going on here?" There's a whole tribe of tree gods who need rehousing. There's a hill Goddess who can't quite sit up owing to the housing estate nestled in her cleavage.

There's a sea Goddess with a rather nasty tummy upset and a wind god screaming, "Whoah! These thermals are too fast. Any chance somebody could turn the heat down? A sun God cries, "Don't blame me." A moon Goddess meanwhile breathes a long drawn-out sigh and asks, "What are we to do?"

If you listen you'll hear them. Their voices chime in the stirring leaves of the oak. We hear their whispers in the waves that beat our shores. When we visit ancient sacred sites and lie down and dream, we may be blessed with their presence and an urgent bidding to protect their gifts.

In return these Gods and Goddesses smile favourably upon us. We can call on them to influence the outcome of wars, love affairs, marriage, childbirth, death, fertility, even homework. Yes, there really is a goddess of schoolchildren. .

So, is the moon more likely to be a God or a Goddess? I refer to the moon as she. But I do think there's a cool man in that moon, just as the fiery passion of a woman radiates from the sun. There is no reason to assume that either the sun or the moon is strictly masculine or feminine. There is, after all, a moon god called Men.

But when we do look to God - any god – we must always remember the Goddess. For her – their – presence allows us to articulate the obvious: women, although different, are equal to men. Female deities are just as plausible as male gods.

In this book I tend to refer to God and Goddess, rather than mention particular deities by name. But you are welcome to include specific Gods if their stories and associations inspire you. On page 226 I've listed some of my favourites which might appeal to you. But there are plenty more. Go exploring.

## Altars

In some faiths altars are associated with formal places of worship. But for others they are as important in the home as a hearth. Indeed the altar and the hearth were once one and the

same thing. Candles placed on altars suggest this link with fire. Many people still place family photographs on the mantelpiece, not realizing that they are continuing the ancient custom of depicting the family above the hearth to offer protection.

The television has recently replaced the hearth as the heart of many homes. It takes pride of place in the main room of the house with all the furniture pointing that way. What a thing to worship!

Refocus your own room with an altar. If you don't have a mantelpiece, a shelf or small table will be fine, or even a windowsill. What you include on your altar may vary with the seasons and the occasion.

I dedicate my altar to Asa and Akasha. Asa is a collective name for all the Norse Gods and I use it to describe every Deity, by whatever name, who has ever been deemed responsible for creation. Akasha means Spirit, essence, karma, the threefold law – even Father Christmas's list of who's been naughty and nice, in a way. Akasha is a Hindu expression for a vast library in the sky which keeps a note of every activity and its effects on everything else.

Asa and Akasha together, therefore, may symbolize the creation of the earth, eternal life on earth (if we don't blow it) and the interconnectedness of all things. When we worship at the altar to Asa and Akasha we give praise, thanks, offerings, prayers and spells for now and our future, every living thing's future and the Elements which support life.

This means you can follow the religious path of your parents and still have an altar to

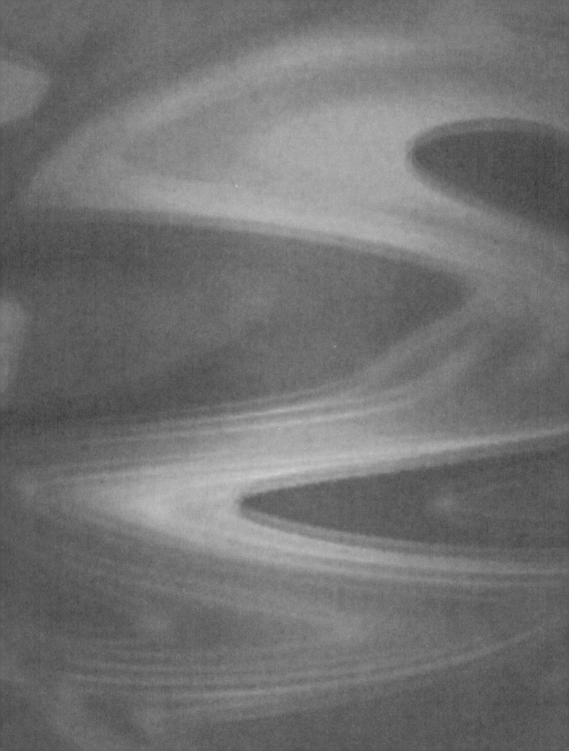

# Symbols for an altar

**Earth** plants, flowers, potpourri, crystals, stones and pebbles, wooden and earthenware bowls, pentacles (made from wicker, wood, clay or wax)
**Air** spiral seashells, incense, oil burner and oils, feathers
**Fire** candles, images of the sun, a wand
**Water** shells, driftwood, a water bowl for floating candles, vases of water for flowers, a cauldron
**Gods** a green man, image of the sun and stars, seeds, nuts, red, orange and yellow flowers
**Goddesses** corn dollies, images of the moon, fruits, blue, white and pink flowers
**Akasha** spiders' webs, mazes, spirals

Other potentially relevant objects include images of family, trees, sunsets and sunrises, rainbows, peace doves, endangered species, your favourite deities and your lunar calendar placed nearby.

Asa and Akasha without feeling you're being disloyal. I know some Gods have been quoted as saying you should ignore all other deities. But they were probably referring to things like oil, weapons and money rather than our living world. No religious teaching says don't respect nature. Quite the opposite, in fact.

The best altar decorations consist of natural objects found or given, rather than bought. They're spell ingredients. Shells you pick up on a beach, flowers grown in your own garden, crystals, photographs you've taken. Religious totems from your own family's faith, such as rosary beads, can also be added, if you feel comfortable with that.

To be complete, your altar should carry symbols of the Elements and Spirit. The table on the left might help.

# An altar ritual

Light some incense – myrrh is good. Light a beeswax candle. Place a cup of wine on the altar and some greenery – a pot plant is perfect. If your altar is above an open fireplace and you're allowed to light a fire in it, do so.

Kneel before your altar. If working with others substitute "we" for "I".

Say, "To Asa and Akasha, soul of nature who gives life to the universe, from whom all things proceed. I give thanks for the air, for the warmth of the sun, the pull of the moon, for the fruits of the earth, the rivers and seas. Let all who share in your precious bounty care, knowing as we do that we share one breath, we have one sun, we have one moon, we walk one earth and we all live downstream."

Take a sip of the wine and drink to our future. Acknowledge that if everyone did their bit, our lives could be transformed.

# Wand

Hazel if you can find it. Choose what you wish, but I choose hazel. It is the wood of wisdom. Some witches prefer willow or ash. Wands are personal things. Often the wand finds you. Please do not harm any tree when obtaining your wand. If it is meant to be, the tree will have already decided to give you a wand and you will find a suitable twig or branch lying close by the trunk, on the ground.

# Expose yourself to the elements

Allowing our bodies and senses to experience the Elements is invigorating and beautifying. "There's no hairdresser better than an onshore wind," says one witch at the drop-in coven I frequent. It's true. Salt air gives tendrils a wild bushiness rich with energy. Rain softens and smooths even the most flyaway of hair. The sun will kiss your locks with natural highlights and the earth provides many treatments to repair damage caused by excess exposure.

It's not just hair that benefits from moderate airing, earthing, watering and warming. Our skin and our beings will both be grateful. So when there's summer rain or a raging storm, strong gales or falling snow, get out and taste it, see it, hear it, smell it, touch it. Feel it.

Just make sure you're safe. Strong winds can blow trees down and whisk slates off roofs. Storms may be accompanied by lightning. So no tree hugging or taking shelter under the tallest tree for miles. In fact, never shelter from a storm under a tree.

But don't let the dangers that inevitably lurk within the Elements scare you too much. They are powerful. Respect their power, utilize their power for good and hopefully the Elements will respect you. Whatever some humans think, it is not our world, this is the Elements' world. They are the world. We are their guests, their children.

On the opposite page are just a few suggestions, courtesy of the drop-in coven, for enjoying the elements. Depending on the amount of privacy you are afforded, you may wish to go naked. It certainly adds to the moment. But don't freeze yourself. On many occasions going barefoot or wearing a swimming costume will be enough. When it's cold, get yourself wrapped up in natural fibres.

Some of these ideas may have to wait until you're old enough to roam where you please. But your parents might like some of them and want to join in. Ask them.

○ Swim in a pool at the bottom of a waterfall.

○ Stand on a hill during a gale. Hold your arms out – and a cloak or cape if you have one – and lean into the wind. It's like flying.

○ Practise tai-chi at dawn.

○ Light a driftwood fire on a beach at sunset.

○ Dance in summer rain.

○ Build a snow Goddess.

○ Grow a herb garden (see page 25).

○ Learn to sail a boat or paddle a canoe (under trained supervision).

○ Visit a volcano (safely under supervision for all ages).

○ Dip your toes in a stream.

○ Take a wander through a forest. Sit down and listen.

○ Hug a tree.

○ Wash your face in dew.

○ Stop and smell the flowers.

○ Go fly a kite.

○ Moonbathe and gaze at the stars.

○ Leave a bedroom window open at night to be awoken by the dawn chorus.

○ Go camping (see page 216).

○ Build sand pyramids on the beach (less militaristic than castles).

○ Learn to surf.

# A herb garden

My friends know I have two obsessions in life. One is the use of plastic shopping bags. I *hate* them and generally tell people so. My other passion is herbs.

My herb garden is a sanctuary, a place of communion. I cannot help but marvel at popping a seed in a pot or in the ground, feeding it a balance of the Elements and whoosh. Life! And how!

That's all there is to gardening, by the way. Plant your seeds in healthy soil, give them warmth, water and air and they grow. Magic!

The shades, textures, colours, scents, tastes, insects, the thought of faeries, enormous gratitude to the Gods. It all goes on in and around my herb garden.

Visitors find it uplifting. Often it seems that something of their presence remains. When my friend Mickey was ill (this book is dedicated to him), he'd sit and watch me weed. I'd lob various herbs to him to sniff or suck. When I want to be close to him, these memories draw me to the herb garden. I miss him. When he was in hospital and later at the hospice I would bring herbal tussie-mussies to him, great bunches of healing energies which he kept by his bed so he could press his face into them when the going was tough – which it was. When the time came I made a wreath for him using these same herbs. There's no end to their uses.

Party drinks, summer salads, herbal sachets for keeping bugs at bay, seasonings, decorations. Herbs do them all.

When choosing which herbs to grow consider their usefulness and their preferred growing conditions. Most like dry soil and sunny conditions but some will tolerate, or prefer, partial shade. Angelica, sweet woodruff, lemon verbena, honeysuckle and evening primrose, among others, are happy in partial shade.

If you don't have a garden, you can grow chives, basil and coriander very well on windowsills. If you have outdoor window-boxes you can also grow thyme and sage. Large tubs are happy homes for mint (on its own, otherwise it takes over), rosemary, hyssop, lavender and bay.

If you can persuade your parents to give you a plot, you can grow any herb. If you have a choice of places, check out where sunlight and shade fall. Go for the spot which receives the most direct sunlight. This will charge up the magical healing properties of your herbs.

Before rushing out and buying the first herbs you find, try to visit a few established herb gardens – historical houses, public gardens and monasteries are a good bet. This will help you to visualize your plans.

You will need to read up, so go find some herb and general gardening books. I've recommended a couple at the back of this one.

Meanwhile, listed over the page are a few herbs which are lovely to have around and useful, too. When you meet these plants, squeeze the leaves and smell. Some will draw you, excite or soothe you, more than others. These are the plants for you.

**Chamomile** (*Anthemis nobilis*) soothes the nerves and tummy when you drink an infusion of flowers.

**Rosemary** (*Rosmarinus officinalis*) aids memory, strong cooking flavour, good for wreathes.

**Lavender** (*Lavandula officinalis*), the all-purpose healer, can be used to flavour honey and is a moth- and flea-repellent.

**Thyme** (*Thymus vulgaris*) – butterflies love it, great for sore throats and flavouring food.

**Sage** (*Salvia officinalis*), the plant of wisdom, good in food, beautiful flowers.

**Tansy** (*Tanacetum vulgare*) flavours omelettes and repels moths and flies – hang a bunch in the kitchen.

**Fennel** (*Foeniculum vulgare*) grows huge, soothes the tummy, tastes great and I've had success with it in birth spells. The seeds, drunk as a tea, encourage breast-milk production.

**Coriander** (*Coriandrum sativum*) – the leaves flavour soups and other dishes, as do the ground seeds. The Egyptians thought coriander protected the soul and placed it in tombs.

**Lemon verbena** (*Aloysia triphylla*) – the happy drug. It fizzes with uplifting sherbet-tasting energy. Perfect for a tea or pot-pourri.

**Lemon balm** (*Melissa officinalis*) – bees love it, older women love it. Perfect for hot flushes. I use it in tussie-mussies, salads and drinks.

Whatever plants you choose, once they're in, we reap our pleasure from tending them in all weathers. Soft drizzle and herbs are a splendid combination with only one exception: rue. When it's wet, water on the plant contains some of its oils which can bring you up in a rash. For this reason I grow rue in a different bed, protected by rose bushes where no one can brush against it.

## To make an infusion

Use 25g /1oz of fresh leaves, flowers and stems (1 tablespoon of dried) to 500ml/1 pint of not quite boiling water. Pour over the herbs in a teapot and leave for 15 minutes.

## To dry herbs

Pick on a dry sunny day when the flowers are just opening. Some time around the summer solstice (about 21 June if you live in the northern hemisphere, 21 December in the southern) is normally perfect, weather permitting. Choose the time of the full moon if you can. The herbs need to dry as rapidly as possible to preserve the oils. Airing cupboards or near an aga will do it. Tie in small bunches and hang them up. When dry they'll feel crisp to the touch. They may now be broken up and stored in old jars with air-tight lids. (A good use for old jars! Better than throwing them into landfill sites or incinerators. Better even than recycling.)

## Essential oils

Essential oils are pure magic in a bottle. Distilled from a variety of herbs and plants, some relax, some balance while others stimulate. Many are antiseptic and others have anaesthetic properties. They are not tested on animals, so they're perfect for vegetarians and vegans plus everyone else who cares about vivisection (experimenting on animals). Some of my favourites are listed over the page.

## Some common essential oils

○ **Lavender**   Relaxing, antiseptic, aids sleep. Following minor burns, scolds, cuts and grazes rinse the wound under the cold tap, then apply neat oil to the skin (lavender is the only oil apart from tea tree that can be applied neat). For earache, a few drops on a warm wet flannel may be used as a compress. Sit in a bowl of water containing a few drops of lavender oil to relieve cystitis.

○ **Coriander**   Stimulating. Good for a body scrub prior to exams, especially an art exam, since it induces creativity and and positive thoughts.

○ **Sweet fennel**   Stimulating, aids digestion, antiseptic. One drop in a glass of water will ensure healthy gums. Heat it on a burner, or wipe on candles following a blow-out meal. Once they've inhaled guests may demand a second helping of pudding. (It also stops you farting!)

○ **Thyme**   Balancing, antiseptic. Use a few drops in warm water to wipe kitchen surfaces, bathrooms, toilets and anything else you require sterile.

○ **Bergamot**   Uplifting, antidepressant, tanning. Mixed with oil and applied to skin it will encourage tanning but will not protect from burning. Good for putting on the burner at parties or when you discover your exams didn't go as well as anticipated.

○ **Geranium**   Balancing, relieving pain, promoting harmony. Can be used as a hot or cold compress on aches and sprains. In massage it relieves anxiety. When heated on a burner it brings calm to a room.

○ **Tea tree**  Stimulating, antiseptic, antifungal. A few drops in a bowl of water make a good anti-spot rinse. Apply neat to athlete's foot and mix with water to spray shoes and wash socks to prevent re-infection. It also cures cold sores. As soon as you get the tingle, apply it neat. It may also be used like thyme oil.

Some oils, such as jasmine or rose, are a tad expensive, but they're still cheaper than designer perfumes. And since they're highly concentrated, a few drops go a long way. Often these rare oils (it takes masses of flowers to produce them) are sold in 5ml bottles instead of the standard 10ml to make them more accessible.

My 5ml of jasmine cost four times more than 10ml of lavender oil. But it's lasted more than four times as long because lavender is more useful. So it gets used more. Jasmine is reserved for luxurious treats when I need cheering up (like after I've waited to cross the road and counted 25 cars all with just one person in them).

The all-round talents of lavender oil make it the perfect choice for newcomers to aromatherapy. You can try others as you prepare for spells and experiment with blends (mixing more than one oil for a specific effect).

In time you'll have your favourites while other people might use different oils to meet similar needs. This is as it should be – since oils influence our emotions and thoughts, they're very personal. Enjoy discovering what works for you.

There are many more oils available than I have space to mention here and they have many more applications than I can describe. See the useful reading list for books which will tell you more.

## Essential Tips

○ Oils can be heated on burners, mixed with carrier oils for massage and body scrubs, added to baths (occasionally – we don't want to waste water, do we?), used in compresses, wiped onto candles or mixed with water for sterilizing purposes.

○ For massage, use one drop of essential oil to 2ml of carrier oil. If aged 12 or under, however, or if you have a sensitive skin, use one drop to 4 ml.

○ A carrier oil is something like sweet almond, olive, sunflower or wheatgerm oil, used to dilute the essential oil.

○ Epileptics should avoid fennel, eucalyptus and basil.

○ Diabetics should avoid eucalyptus, geranium and lemon.

○ Candles should be wiped with a warm damp cloth before oils are applied.

○ Oil burners require hot water mixed with the oils. Ensure the dish doesn't burn dry.

○ In baths, use no more than five drops. Swish them around, wait a couple of minutes, then climb in. The oils can be mixed with alcohol or oil first, but they don't have to be.

## Breathing

Breathing deeply and thoughtfully is good. So long as you're not breathing in fumes, it relaxes, energizes and clears the mind. Prior to a spell, or any potentially stressful situation, breathe well and you will be better able to achieve what you expect of yourself.

Sitting on a straight-backed chair, hands on

llap, palms facing upwards and feet on the ground, or sitting comfortably on the floor, cross-legged, close your eyes. Breathe out through your mouth for seven counts if you can manage it. Start with three or five if you can't.

Hold it there for seven counts. (By hold, I mean neither breathe in nor breathe out.) Now breathe in through your nose for seven counts, hold for seven counts, breathe out for seven counts, hold for seven counts.

Do this until you feel calm and collected. Always breathe in through your nose and out through your mouth.

You can, having breathed out for seven, breathe out again instead of holding. This will rid your lungs of more carbon dioxide and provide room for more oxygen. Give it a go. Your blood loves this exchange.

To help you achieve breaths of seven, as I call them, allow your ribs to expand as you breathe in. Squeeze the air out by pulling and pushing up your diaphragm (the muscle below your ribcage).

To gauge how much extra oxygen you've given yourself, when you've been doing the exercise for a minute or two (it doesn't take long), wait after your out breath. Don't force it, but count how long it takes before your body decides to breathe in. See? Your oxygen tank is filled. Compare this to the panting your body insists on after strenuous exercise.

Now you are equipped with the basic tools you're ready to begin.

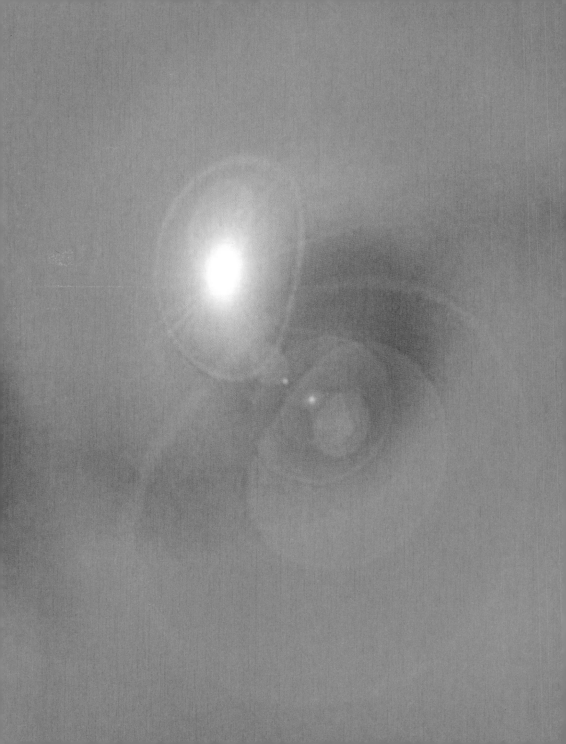

A healthy mind, body and spirit are essential to a happy fulfilling life. To achieve this is simple enough in itself. But it may require you to change your habits of a life time. It will involve approaching the most basic of needs in ways you might not have thought of. Have a go. By focusing on these seven different aspects of your life, you will find it transformed. You – and the rest of the world – will be healthier and happier and your spells will definitely work better.

# Your health matters

# For a healthy mind, body and spirit

*YOU WILL NEED:*

**nourishment**
**liquid**
**exercise**
**relaxation**
**kindness**
**respect**
**a clear conscience**

## Nourishment

Three meals a day may well keep hunger at bay, but unless we eat the right mixture of foods, we starve ourselves of the essential nutrients which are the building blocks of life. Without these we may experience poor concentration, lethargy and be prone to all sorts of ailments which lead to emotional and physical stress. And let's face it, who needs that?

Fortunately Mother Nature ensures our fabulous world is able (for now) to provide every nurturing nutrient we could ever possibly need, in the West at least.

When we eat in a way that respects Nature's cycles and intricate ecosystems, not only do we reap the physical health benefits, we promote spiritual well-being also. In fact, our diet is so important that it has a chapter to itself, starting on page 48.

## Liquids

Do you drink at least 1.5 litres/3 pints of tap water every day? We need more than 2 litres/3½ pints a day. Since most foods contain water we get some liquid intake just by eating. But we still need to drink plenty of water as well. It is essential for good concentration, the complexion, regulating body temperature, purifying the blood and generally keeping our internal organs in tip-top condition.

Every day 25,000 people worldwide die because they don't have access to clean drinking water. That's two million humans every year. And yet so many of us fail to appreciate the value of the life force that comes gushing out of our taps at the twist of a knob. We waste it.

Drinking water is an easy cheap way to improve our general condition. If you really don't like the taste, try herbal teas instead. For ecological reasons, avoid bottled water. They're part of the great nonsense that got the world in this mess in the first place.

The bottled water industry leaves us with mountains of plastic and nowhere to put it. Transporting water in bottles rather than pipes adds to the traffic on our roads. In some countries bottled water is sold while the local drinking water is polluted by the production of....er....plastic, plus farming and industry.

It's water we need, straight out of the tap or the well. Not plastic.

There has been much discussion as to the healthiness of tap water. In London, for instance, it has been revealed that each glass of water has been through seven sets of kidneys before it comes out of your tap. It is a rather yucky thought. But at the same time we have to remember that we only have so much water on this planet. I'm sure the water we drink has seen many more kidneys than seven. It's been through all the dinosaurs' kidneys as well!

What we should think seriously about, though, is the pollution our water contains. Some of it is from medicines and tablets, such as antibiotics and the pill women take to avoid pregnancy. Some of it is the chemicals we use to make our sinks and toilets sparkle. The rest comes from industry and farming.

Many sources of bottled water will contain similar levels of pollution to tap water. It might come from a well, but where do you suppose the well gets its water from? Correct. The water table. The same source as water from taps. The only way to remove this pollution is to treat it with more chemicals (deemed far too expensive by the water companies) or not pollute our water in the first place.

The best compromise to be reached so far is the use of filters on drinking-water taps. You can also use a filtered jug. Just remember to change the filter regularly. This prevents a build-up of contaminants such as germs. And chemicals.

# Relaxation

Sitting on a beach with the sun setting, the moon rising and the rhythmic sound of waves lulling me into a dream-like state is my ideal form of relaxation. It de-stresses and enthuses. I like pottering around in my herb garden, too. Whatever presses your relaxation buttons is good to do. So long as it leaves a minimal eco-footprint (see Respect, page 40, if you don't know what that means) and is relaxing, rather than just switching to zombie mode.

For when you are relaxing, you have given yourself permission to stop worrying about what you've done and shouldn't have done and how much time you don't have to fit in all the things you should have done. I know, it's a nightmare, which is why relaxation is so important.

Yoga and meditation might be appropriate. I think it's best to get a bit of qualified tuition before branching out alone in your bedroom. Evening classes can be quite cheap and you may well get a discount if you're in full-time

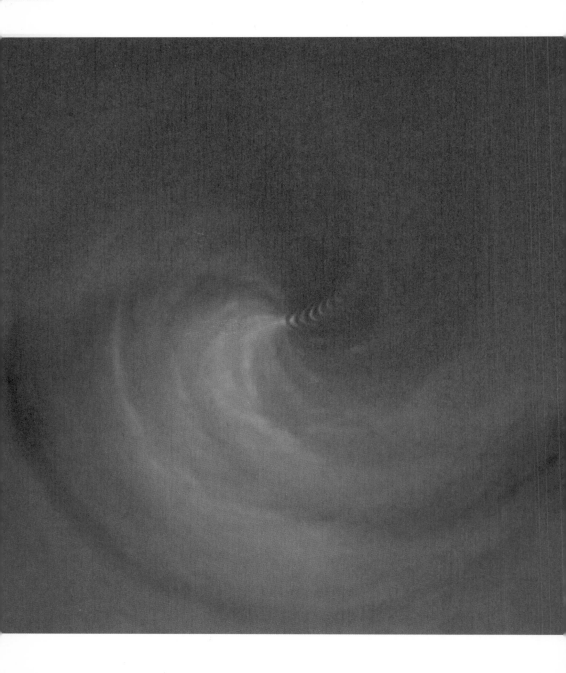

education. Your local library is likely to be a good source of information.

Recent research has shown that Buddhist monks really are happier after meditation – a happiness that stays with them throughout the day. Yoga fans will tell you that they feel fitter in body and soul after regular practice.

# Note to self

Relaxing is not the same as lazing around. TV watching might feel like relaxing but the long-term effects are more harmful than healthful. Witches don't watch much TV. It uses a lot of electricity and it's so passive. Spend an evening watching TV and it's often difficult to remember what you've seen. You switch it on, then switch yourself off. Witches prefer to read books, do the crossword or garden. And party!

# Exercise

Sports, dancing, running, gardening, cycling, climbing, walking, swimming, housework. It's all exercise. And it is one of the most powerful good deeds you can treat yourself to. Regular exercise will encourage a good night's sleep and a healthy appetite, improve concentration and ensure you simply ooze with an endless supply of magical energy.

After a few weeks of exercise, instead of slouching from class to class, you'll have teachers shouting, "Walk, don't run" in your wake, you'll be learning to cook and finding that although you may be spending less time studying, you're actually able to take more information in.

Due to our increasingly mechanized world, human beings are falling out of the habit of taking routine doses of exercise. This has alarming implications. We're evolving into an overweight, slothful species suffering from all manner of ills, from heart disease and diabetes to obesity, which could all be easily avoided – if only we'd get up off our backsides and get the blood pumping round our systems.

The following tips might help get you started:

● Turn off the TV and go for a walk or a bike ride instead.

● When using buses, spurn the nearest stop and walk to the next one.

● Avoid lifts or elevators. Take the stairs (at least some of the way).

● At the shopping mall or underground station, walk up and down the escalators.

● Organize a sponsored walk for charity.

● Dust off your old costume and head for your nearest swimming pool.

● Join a dance class.

● Learn a new sport.

● Plant up your own herb or vegetable garden, then maintain it.

● Try to do a few simple exercises every day such as sit-ups, press-ups and stretches. Set yourself targets, such as 20 sit-ups without stopping each morning by the end of the week. Then beat your own target. You'll love what it does to your tummy, bottom and thighs.

● Offer to walk dogs for elderly relatives, friends and neighbours. You might even be able to earn a little bit of pocket money out of it. Don't forget to scoop the poop, though.

# Sleep

We spend a third of our lives sleeping and a good proportion of this appears to be done in our teen years. But how often are you lying in bed not sleeping at all? You toss and turn, kept awake by worry. Or you wake early, maybe after a bad dream, and you don't get up because you just can't face the day?

If this is a good description of your sleeping patterns, there's plenty you can do to improve things. We need sleep because that's when we do most of our growing, replenish cells and tissues, and get our brains in order. This "downtime" is necessary to process all the information we accumulate while we're awake.

A good night's sleep does wonders for our academic prowess, improves our mood and provides the vitality and strength needed to make the most of life.

To ensure your sleep is long enough – 10 hours should do it when you're growing, though most adults manage on eight or less – and deep enough, try these tips:

● Avoid caffeine-laden drinks such as tea, coffee and cola in the evening (actually, avoid cola altogether). Try chamomile tea instead.
● Try the a-maze-ing problem solver on page 177.
● Get plenty of fresh air and exercise. You'll be asleep before you've taken off your trainers.
● Avoid spicy foods and heavy meals late in the evening. Indigestion can play havoc with sleep routines.
● Heat 5 drops of lavender or chamomile oil in a burner in your bedroom before bedtime.
● Make a herbal pillow.

● Go flying. It's such a fascinating activity and you don't need a besom (broomstick). Lie in bed and close your eyes. Gather together your spirit, the bit of you that is of your mind rather than body. It's your imagination, your thoughts, your dreams, your character, your emotions, the inner you. Allow this bit of yourself to rise up above your body and see how the room looks from that angle. Continue upwards, through the ceiling and keep going until you end up on your roof. Now you can take flight anywhere you wish. Concentrate on being able to see what's down below, be it roof

## To make a herbal pillow

**a selection of dried herbs: hops, lavender, chamomile flowers and marjoram**
**2 squares or circles of muslin cloth**
**a needle and thread**

Sew the cloth pieces together, leaving a gap so that you can stuff it with the herbs, then sew up the gap. Herb pillows can be decorated with ribbons, lace and embroidery – it doesn't have to look like something Granny would like, though. You could always embroider a big CND sign in multi-coloured thread or a pentacle in silver.

Add a few drops of essential oil occasionally to maintain the soporific effect of your herb pillow. But be mindful to choose relaxing rather than stimulating oils. Cedarwood, frankincense and sandalwood are all suitable, as is lavender, which is readily available.

tops and gardens, woodland, farmland or the coast. Now off you go, young witch. Go exploring. I swear you'll be asleep before you've finished your journey, but you'll wake up back in your body
⊙ Read a book – preferably not one on your school reading list. Read up on ancient deities or herbal remedies. Avoid cookery books at such times. While they can be fascinating reads, they do tend to make you hungry, which won't help you sleep at all.

## Kindness

You will be amazed at how good you feel after helping someone. This feel-good factor gives us greater confidence which improves our performance, whatever the task. Try it. Shop for an elderly person or help them feed their zillion pet cats. Take time to listen to someone's problems and find a way to cheer them up. Open a door for someone, give something away to a person you know will appreciate it, undertake some voluntary work for an environmental charity or give your parents a break in some way. There are more ways to be kind than there are cats owned by old ladies. It's true.

## Respect

Having respect means understanding your needs as well as everyone else's.

Respect yourself by caring for your health. Respect the needs of others through politeness and going out of your way to help when you can.

Respect your surroundings in all you do. Leave the faintest of eco-footprints on your journey through life. An eco-footprint is what results from your activities. If you walk to a field, lie down and listen to the whisper of the grass, the eco-footprint is minimal. If you drive to an airport to visit a country far away that specializes in creating an environment similar to home, the eco-footprint becomes a rather large stomp.

In return, you will be respected. By others as thoughtful as yourself and by future generations. In a hundred years, when people your age are busy with their history or environmental studies, they'll be able to put down their books and say, "Now that generation made a difference. They were good ancestors. Respect!"

## A clear conscience

We all sleep and feel better when our lives are free from guilt. Turn to page 80 for a spell to help clean up your conscience. You might want to read through the easy-peasy tips for saving the Elements and Spirit first, though (see pages 82-92).

However, none of us can be healthy all the time, however much we look after ourselves, so turn the page for…

# A few remedies for common ailments

## Asthma

Asthma sucks. Increasingly common among the young, it may be caused by anything from food intolerance to a cat allergy. Pollution, especially from car exhausts, certainly exacerbates the problem.

Those who suffer know how important it is to keep their medicine with them at all times. But if you want to head off attacks at the pass, as 'twere, try to keep stress levels to a minimum. This involves controlling your frame of mind: simply refuse to be upset by everyday annoyances and do your best to take big things, like exams, in your stride. Yeah, right.

The following herbal remedies should prove helpful in soothing stress and helping you to breathe easily. Please use these in conjunction with your normal medication since they are to ease symptoms rather than to provide a total cure. With luck, you may grow out of your asthma some time during your teen years.

## Breathe easy Tea

**at least 1 lemon balm bush**
**hot water**

Grow the plant from seed (very easy – just follow the instructions on the packet) or buy an organic plant from a herb specialist. Grow it in a large container and you're free to house it outside in summer and bring it indoors over winter to provide leaves all year round.

Take 75g/3oz of fresh leaves (if using dried leaves use just 25g/1oz – see page 26 for how to dry herbs). Place the herb in a glass or ceramic teapot and pour in 500ml/1 pint of hot, not boiling water (allow it to go off the boil). Brew for 10 minutes. Using a tea strainer, pour out a mugful and drink it. Put the rest in a flask to keep it warm. Drink a glass or mugful three times a day.

Make it fresh, daily.

## Benzoin lung lightener

This is particularly useful on days when stress is bound to raise its ugly head. Exams, exam results, sporting fixtures and visits from relatives. You know what gets your goat. Use this healing aid first thing when you rise.

**benzoin oil**
**an oil burner and tealight candle**
**warm water**

A good aromatherapy supplier will be able to sell you benzoin. This thick dark gum-type oil smells rather like vanilla and has been recommended for asthma since the 16th century. It is often a primary ingredient of incense and was once believed to cast off dark spirits. There aren't many things darker than an asthma attack, so give it a go.

Heat up five drops of oil with warm water in your burner. Sit cross-legged on the floor and slowly breathe in the scent (follow the breathing instructions on page 30. Since your lungs may be tight, reduce the number of counts – breathe in for three, hold for three, etc., if you can't manage seven. It will become easier over time.)

As the scent fills the room and your lungs, a warm glow and a loosening of the chest shall come upon you.

## Common cold

We all get them. They make us feel lousy and look worse. Prevention is better than cure. As winter and the cold season approaches, fortify your immune system by eating oodles of fresh raw fruit and lightly steamed vegetables every day while getting plenty of fresh air and exercise. It may not stop you catching colds altogether, but it will help you cast them off more quickly.

When you do go down with a runny nose, watery eyes, sore throat and aching limbs, take to your bed with plenty of handkerchiefs and one of the following remedies. I've included a few in the hopes you will have at least some of these ingredients at home already.

## Cold buster

**1 clove of garlic**
**juice of half a lemon**
**hot water**
**1 teaspoon of honey (or more to taste)**

Chop up the garlic as finely as you have the patience for. Place in a cup with the lemon juice. Add hot water and stir in the honey. Drink while warm, inhaling the steam between sips. When you've finished, scoop up the garlic with a spoon and eat it.

## Sore Throat gargle

**a bunch of thyme**
**a teapot**
**500ml/1 pint of hot but not boiling water**

Crush the thyme leaves, pop them in the teapot, add the water and allow to infuse for 10 minutes or more.

Pour the infusion through a strainer into a cup. Gargle with it. It tastes disgusting, but it works. At least I think it does. I give it to my stepdaughter. She certainly stops complaining about her sore throat. Maybe she'd rather suffer than gargle.

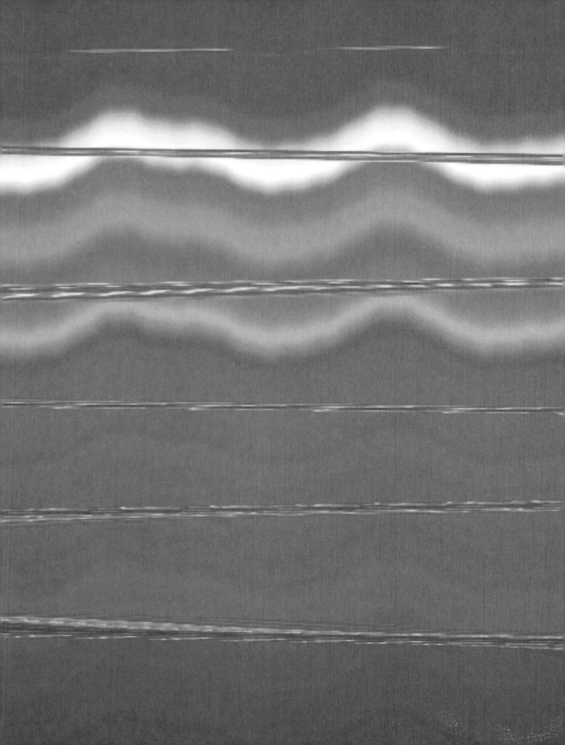

# Steamy nose debunger

**a bunch of crushed mint**
**a bowl**
**a large towel**
**any of the following: a bunch of**
**lemon balm, 3 drops of myrtle oil,**
**7 crushed sage leaves, 3 crushed**
**sprigs of rosemary**
**hot water**

Place the herbs in the bowl and pour on the water. Drape the towel over your head to catch the steam, lean over the bowl and inhale the healing aroma. The water needs to be very hot, so be careful you don't burn yourself with the steam, or the water.

# Achy-shaky foot soak

**hot water**
**a bowl**
**any of the herbs listed in the Steamy**
**Nose Debunger**
**any of the following essential oils (if you**
**mix them, ensure you don't have more**
**than 3 drops altogether): lavender,**
**rosemary, benzoin, sandalwood**

Crush your herbs, pour on the water, add your oils and swish it around. Slip your feet in, sit back and relax until the water cools.

# Emergency relief

There are times when you might want to be tucked up in bed, but it's impossible. This will help.

**a handkerchief**
**eucalyptus oil**

Eucalyptus oil contains properties that both stimulate the body and ease the airways. Place three drops on a handkerchief and sniff when the going gets tough.

# Death to all germs

We should never wish harm on any living organism but we owe the cold virus no favours. This oil blend will kill germs in the air which may stop them spreading to others. It is effective with most airborne nasties, both viral and bacterial.

**5 drops of rosemary oil**

Heat on a burner and the air in the sick room will be purified.

*Try to use handkerchiefs rather than paper tissues – it saves trees*

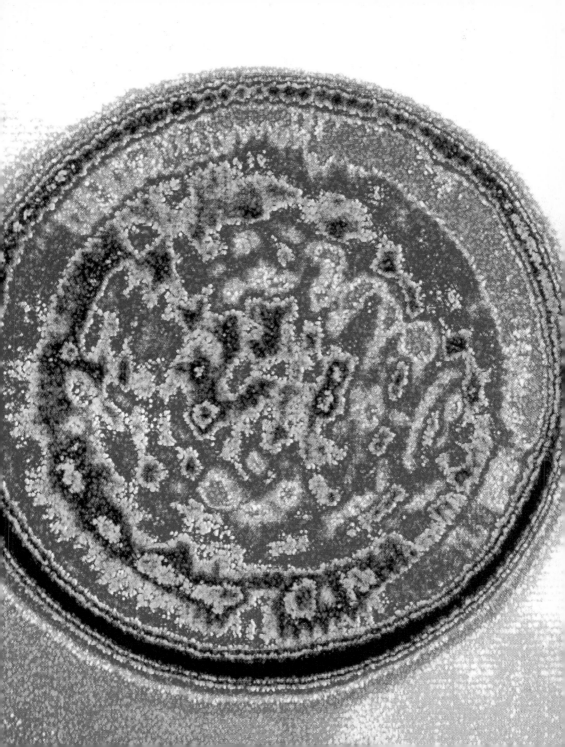

Once you're tall enough to reach the cooker and considered responsible enough to use it, your culinary horizons need know no bounds. Forget those boring old cereals and microwaved nibbles that have long kept you going between proper meals (or….ahem…instead of proper meals).

With a little bit of thought, the most feeble of fare may be transformed into sumptuous snacks, luscious lunches, delicious dinners and superb suppers. And it can be healthy, economical and do very little harm to the planet.

# Food for thought

*SO LONG AS YOU REMEMBER YOU'RE COOKING (THE PHONE RINGS, IT'S YOUR BEST FRIEND, YOU LISTEN, HOURS PASS, THERE'S A BANG ON THE DOOR, YOU HANG UP TO LET THE FIREMEN IN), YOUR FAMILY WILL NO DOUBT DELIGHT IN YOUR NEWFOUND CULINARY SKILLS AND CALL ON YOU CONSTANTLY TO TICKLE THEIR TASTEBUDS. THIS IS NO BAD THING. FOR HE OR SHE WHO COOKS CAN LEAVE THE WASHING UP TO OTHERS. AND THE DRYING.*

## Organic Food

Organic farmers appreciate that Nature can sustain our needs if we treat her with respect. This means we take no more than we need and replace what we can, working with her rather than against her. All forms of flora and fauna are encouraged to thrive alongside crops in a harm-free environment.

This is why (no)alternatives and/or witches choose to eat organic food. I'm sure we're all well rehearsed in the pitfalls of what we call "conventional" methods of farming. When food is mass-produced, profits are deemed more important than the health of the environment and the animals and humans who are destined to eat the products.

To maximize profits, companies rely heavily on the use of chemicals to increase yields. Insects are viewed as the enemy and obliterated, which kills local wildlife as well, either directly from the poisons or because their natural prey is removed from the food chain.

Often the ground is "overworked". Nature can't keep up with our outrageous demands and so chemical fertilizers are used extensively to improve fertility. These pollutants seep and pour into our waterways where they cause untold damage. Fish, amphibians and other forms of wildlife are affected.

The problem is not a localized one for coastal regions. Farms in the Mid West of America, for example, have caused the death of a vast expanse of sea in the Gulf of Mexico. Nothing can survive there any more.

It's not just fish, amphibians, corals (nurseries for the babies of many fish species), micro-organisms, whales, dolphins, insects, birds and small mammals that are threatened by our food-production methods. Farm workers are affected too. Those who apply the chemicals suffer from cancer, Alzheimer's

Heed ye flower, bush and Tree
By The Lady, blessed be
Wiccan Rede

disease and poisoning. Poor farmers in developing countries often spend their meagre profits on medicines to treat these chemical-related conditions.

Sometimes these farmers are paid such low prices for their produce that they make no profits at all and have to rely on aid, just to survive. Meanwhile, for the major food distributors, the profits are increasing all the time. Modern technology means that we know what's going on all round our world. With this knowledge, surely, comes responsibility.

## Genetic modification

If you eat organic food, you can also be sure that it has not been grown from genetically modified (GM) seeds. Among the arguments for genetic modification is the belief that it is good to create plants that are resistant to certain diseases. It means less spraying of crops in the future.

The counter-argument claims that these GM plants could cross-pollinate with non-GM plants. We do not know what effect this could have. It might mean that a lowly weed becomes a superweed (because it too will be immune to certain diseases which have naturally kept its numbers in check). This would lead to more chemical sprays being used in the future, not less.

This is only one line of a debate which is currently raging among scientists, farmers, politicians, (no)alternatives and other consumers. And yet all the while an increasing number of genetically modified crops is being grown around the world.

The argument will be settled eventually, one way or the other. We have to hope the modifiers are right. Because if they're wrong and we all know they're wrong, well, it doesn't bear thinking about. It might be the final GM straw for Nature. Let's hope she won't be feeling vengeful.

This is why many shoppers boycott GM foods, such as soya, cooking oil and tomatoes. If you wish to boycott GM foods – and many of your parents probably already do – look out for labels stating that a product is GM free. All organically certified food is GM free.

## Persuading parents to go organic

Reasons for going organic might make perfect sense to you. But your parents may be less enthusiastic. They might tell you organic food is too expensive, that it is a con and no different from non-organic produce.

It *is* different. It tastes better, keeps better, cooks better, is proven to contain more nutrients and feels better – you know it's been grown with love.

The organic movement is not a con – although I'm sure there are plenty of eager profiteers who would love to get in on the act. Organic growers farm organically because they know it is better for them, their children, the public at large and the environment. No one gets up at 5a.m. to hoe between rows of carrots on a whim. Organic farmers do it

Live and let live - fairly take and fairly give

Wiccan Rede

because they know what's happening and they care.

Organic food can seem expensive. It is bound to. Labour costs more than a barrel of chemicals. But if we think about how we budget our finances, we can save money in other areas of our lives which means we'll have more to spend on organic produce.

If more of us supported smaller stores such as healthfood shops, this would help too. The food won't have travelled so far, because, unlike supermarkets, smaller shops tend to buy local. This cuts the costs of bringing food to the customer. The greater the turnover for these smaller outlets, the more chance they have of bringing the prices down.

A cheaper way still to buy organic is to support local farmers' markets or organize a veg box scheme in your community. These schemes deliver vegetables straight to your door, with the minimum of packaging.

Organic food is cheaper still if you grow some of it yourself. Cucumbers and tomatoes, lettuces and herbs need no more than a bright windowsill. While potatoes and courgettes/zucchini are happy with a sunny balcony or patio.

You could also contribute some of your allowance, or wages from a Saturday job, to the cause.

## Changing over to organics

You don't have to empty the contents of your cupboards and begin afresh. This would be wasteful. But you can start introducing organic produce to your family – while waiting for your seeds to grow – by choosing a few products that you buy regularly, such as bread, butter, cheese, milk and eggs.

As various stocks in the food cupboard like baked beans, cereals, rice, pasta and peanut butter are used up, gradually replace these with an organic alternative.

If the person responsible for the main shop in your household claims to be too busy to go rummaging in search of organics, offer to go along and help out. Or do the shopping yourself. If the primary shopper is so busy, they will hardly refuse your help.

You could also cut down on expensive processed foods and snacks and make sure nothing is wasted. If you cook rice and there's a bit left over in the saucepan, put it in the fridge and make a quick lunch out of it the following day. Just stir-fry a few vegetables and seeds (sesame, sunflower or hemp seeds are good), add the rice (make sure it's piping hot), pour on a bit of shoyu sauce (additive-free soya sauce) and hey presto! Two meals for the price of one. Your parents will love you.

## Note to self

Tantrums and rows will not make my parents see that organic is magic. Gentle persuasion, strategically placed leaflets, my help with the shopping and an organic food festival organized for Earth Day might, though.

# Essential life Tool 2 ✪

## A bicycle

Bikes are clean and green. As we travel we leave no eco-footprints whatsoever in our wake. They're great for tummies, bottoms and thighs, too, and get the heart pumping.

When it comes to causing global warming, cars are the worst offenders on earth. If we could all cut down our journeys by 30km (20 miles) each month we'd have a chance of reversing the damage already done. Avoiding short car trips to the shops for small forgotten items can make a difference. Get on your bike.

Most cities and towns have bike routes and cycle lanes. If your neighbourhood is lacking, start a campaign through your school.

## Cycle sense

◍ Take a cycling proficiency course. These are often organized by the local police. Ask them.

◍ Own a bike pump and puncture repair kit and know how to use them.

◍ Keep your bike well-maintained. Check brakes and oil the chain regularly.

◍ Wear a crash helmet.

◍ Use a face mask in heavy traffic (to protect you from pollution).

◍ After dark, wear reflective strips and make sure your lights work.

## Meat

We need to have a quick chat about meat. Each to their own, but there's nothing I love more, food wise, than knawing meat (lamb preferably, flavoured with rosemary from my herb garden) straight off the bone.

But I have been unable to bring myself to do this of late. I know the destruction caused by the meat industry and the cruelty involved. Animals are penned (caged, really) in dark cramped surroundings before being forced into an even more cramped vehicle to travel miles to the slaughter. They are fed growth hormones and antibiotics which enter our bodies when we eat the meat products.

The phosphate-rich waste from farmed animals pours into our rivers and onwards to the sea, all the while suffocating life. The phosphate causes algae blooms, which prevent oxygen and light from reaching the sea life below. Large tracts of the sea-bed die off and nothing can survive there.

If you want to eat meat, make sure it is organic. That way you know the animals have been treated kindly and not been pumped full of chemicals. Organic meat seems more expensive. But (unlike intensively reared meat) it's not injected with water to increase the weight, which means organic cuts don't shrink so much while cooking and consequently the meat goes further. Eat less meat and you can afford organic meat.

Alternatively, you could become a vegetarian (see page 58).

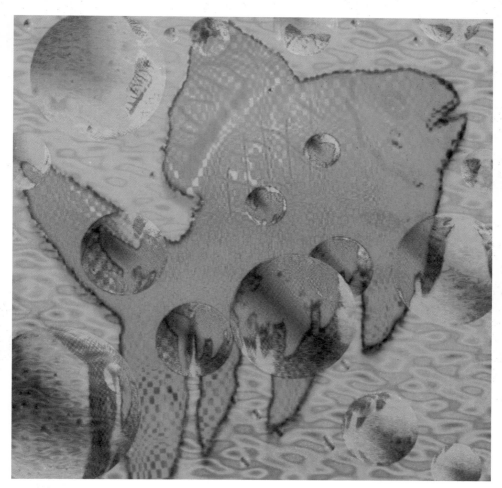

# A fishy business

We need to discuss fish, too. Fish is a staple protein source for many cultures around the world. But ask any fisherman and he will tell you stocks are dangerously low. Once-common species such as cod and haddock are now endangered.

This is because our fisheries have not been managed in a helpful way. Global fishing fleets are 40 per cent larger than our seas and oceans can sustain. This has led to nearly 70 per cent of the world's major marine fish stocks being overfished. Madness!

Because our seas and oceans are so

polluted, there is also a big question mark over the health of the fish that arrives at our table coated in breadcrumbs. Whatever the fish ate, we're eating it too.

These two issues force us to ask a fundamental question: should we be eating fish? Some say eat no fish, it's poisonous. Some say it's not that bad, just don't eat it every day. Some say don't eat any fish. The industry must go. Others say fish caught using dolphin-friendly nets (thousands of dolphins drown from being caught in trawling nets) is okay, but avoid endangered species like cod.

But if the cod is dead and lying on a fishmonger's slab, well it's dead, isn't it? Someone might as well eat it, otherwise it will just be thrown away. Then the cod will have died for nothing. Modern fishing methods mean that most fishermen don't have the chance to spy a cod in the nets, rescue it and throw it back. The nets empty directly into the bowels of the fishing vessel.

So perhaps the answer is only to buy fish from local fishermen using small boats who may well notice when a cod comes up. After all, there's so few fish now, the old boys can often count a catch on their fingers and toes.

This means fish fingers and fillets, scampi, all the mass-produced stuff, are out. This fish is generally caught by huge vessels which vacuum up every sea creature in their path. You don't have to be a marine biologist to work out that this method is unsustainable.

When the fish go, maybe then, as that wise old Native American Chief Seattle once said, we will realize that we cannot eat our money.

# Dairy produce

All cheese, yoghurt and milk should be organic for reasons already mentioned. Eggs too. Free range are more acceptable than battery, but organic layers have a superior quality of life. They are fed organic food and have more freedom to run around. Consequently their eggs taste better. Much better.

Organic eggs cost more, but if you cut down on the number of meat dishes you eat – or cut them out altogether – you can afford to eat a four-egg organic omelette with fresh herbs, served with salad, dressed with homemade herb oil. Oh yes!

# Vegetarianism

It is perfectly possible to survive and flourish on an organic vegetarian diet so long as you take care to ensure you get the right mix of nutrients.

Everyone needs a diet high in carbohydrate with some fat and protein. Without fish and meat, which are high in proteins and fat, you will have to look elsewhere. Fortunately there are plenty of pulses and some vegetables that will meet your needs.

Suitable meals for a vegetarian or anyone else would be wholemeal pasta in a creamy green vegetable sauce; a Spanish omelette, served with vegetables or salad; or rice and lentils with vegetable curry.

The table overleaf shows you suitable sources high in carbohydrates, proteins and fats.

To pep up a meal and increase your protein intake, sprinkle a dish with roasted seeds or dress it with oils which may be flavoured with herbs. The best way to roast seeds is not to roast them at all. Heat a frying pan (no need to use any oil), pour in the seeds and swirl them around for a minute or two. Scrummy.

Sprouted beans are good, too (see page 61).

## Essential life Tool 3 ✪

## Recipe books

Being able to prepare fresh, nutritious, scrummy meals is most definitely an essential life skill. Recipe books are great for explaining the basics and inspiring you to try different ingredients. So start collecting. You can often find piles of them in charity shops.

## Convincing Mum you want to be a vegetarian

When you announce you're becoming a vegetarian, Mum is entitled to groan. After all, isn't it her who has to cook for everyone? "Not another individual meal," she sighs. It is tempting, for the sake of convenience, to eat what the rest of the family eats, minus the fish or meat. But a diet of vegetables alone is unlikely to provide you with all the essential nutrients.

With your parents' support, perhaps you can mix and match, sharing some of their food while supplementing your diet with vegetarian staples like miso soup. (Miso is a paste made from rice and soya beans. Pop a spoonful in a cup and just add hot water, or create a wholesome soup adding vegetables to a miso stock.) Healthfood shops stock everything a vegetarian might need, since veggies are their most dedicated customers.

Dairy produce will also provide protein and fats, but too much of these and the weight may begin to pile on. Unless you're active.

Other valuable sources of protein and fats include peanut butter, tahini (a paste made from sesame seeds which tastes great in sauces), bean and seed sprouts and seed oils.

An avocado and alfalfa sprout sandwich or a peanut butter and fair trade banana butty are excellent snacks. The bread should be wholemeal.

There is a danger, particularly with teenage girls, that a vegetarian diet could cause anaemia, through lack of iron. So make sure you eat plenty of the following: tofu, beans

| | |
|---|---|
| **Carbohydrates** | wholemeal bread, pasta, noodles, rice, beans (all types), lentils, potatoes, oats, cereals (e.g. barley), fruits and vegetables. |
| **Proteins** | eggs, cheese, milk and other dairy produce, peas, beans, pulses and wholegrains, tofu and other soya sources such as soya milk, rice, houmous, beansprouts, wholegrains and potatoes. |
| **Fats** | (there are three types: saturated, poly-unsaturated and mono-unsaturated. Saturated fats should be limited since large amounts can lead to heart disease. The others are good for you.): milk, cheese, butter, natural yoghurt, crème fraîche, fromage frais, hemp seeds and hemp-seed oil, linseed oil, olive oil, sunflower oil, nuts and nut oils, avocados, tofu. |

and pulses, spinach, cabbage, whole grains, parsley, dried fruits (apricots, prunes and dates) and pumpkin seeds.

If you can maintain pre-vegetarian energy and health levels – or improve upon them – I can't see why your parents will have any complaints, especially when they work out how much money you're saving them. Beans and pulses, even organic ones, are cheaper than non-organic meat.

Whenever we change our diets, it should be done gradually, over a few weeks. Months even. This helps your body and digestive system to acclimatize to the biggest change in its life.

Have a go. You never know, even Dad may develop an addiction to your sunflower, hemp and sesame seed sprout mix.

# To sprout beans and seeds

It is far cheaper to sprout your own and involves less packaging than shop-bought supplies. They put old jam jars to good use, too.

Choose either alfalfa seeds, aduki beans, sesame seeds, sunflower seeds, hemp seeds or mung beans (commonly used in Chinese food). I often sprout a mixture together.

Wash the seeds thoroughly, put in a clean jar, cover with cold water and soak overnight. In the morning, drain and cover the jar opening with a piece of fine cloth (muslin is good) and secure with a rubber band.

Rinse the seeds three times a day and keep well drained (lying the jar on its side helps).

Within three to six days you will have a delicious, vitamin-packed food. Store in the fridge and consume within three days.

# Herb oils

These make can make the limpest of salads sit up and sparkle. They're also high in healthy fats and protein and, again, are a good way to reuse old bottles and jars. Plus, they make great gifts.

Use olive, sunflower or hemp-seed oil. Add a good bunch of the following herbs: thyme, rosemary, sage and garlic. Chillis can also be used. Crush them slightly and add to the oil. Store on a windowsill, shaking them up every day. After two weeks, your oils will be brimming with flavour and ready to use. Remove the old herbs (by straining) and add fresh herbs.

For lemon-flavoured oil, use lemon verbena, lemon balm and slices of lemon

# Breakfast

This is the most important meal of the day for veggies and non-veggies alike. Without a hearty start to the day, you'll be flagging by lunchtime. Your concentration will be poor and later you won't feel like taking part in anything more active than searching for your TV remote control.

A good witch begins each day mixing and matching the following:

**Bowl of porridge** Soaking the oats in water overnight means they will take just a couple of minutes to cook. Bring to the boil and simmer, stirring all the time. Add milk once the porridge is in the bowl and immediately soak the saucepan in water (this makes it soooooooo much easier to clean, especially if you're not washing up until the evening). Porridge can be sweetened with dried fruit (also soaked in water overnight) or fresh fruit.

**Muesli** You can mix up your own or buy it from a healthfood shop. Avoid the stuff in cereal boxes, which is often high in sugar. Muesli consists of rolled oats, bran, nuts and dried or fresh fruit. Delicious served with a topping of natural yoghurt.

**Wholemeal toast** Use butter – I do. So long as it's kept at room temperature (in a butter dish) rather than in the fridge, it will spread pretty thinly. Add peanut butter, a yeast extract like Marmite or Vegemite, or cream cheese.

Experiment with fruit additions (peanut butter and apple? Yes, please).

**Fruit salad** A few portions can be made together. Stored with a lid in a fridge, fruit salad lasts for at least three days – unless your family can't resist. So make plenty.

Choose organic banana, apple, peach, pear, citrus, kiwi, pineapple, grapes – whatever you love that is available. Seasonal and local are best. Chop them up chunky style and add some apple juice. If you soak apples in lemon juice before hand, they won't go brown. Top off with natural yoghurt and a sprinkle of muesli.

**Liquids** Drink plenty of water and herbal teas (lemon verbena or peppermint are good morning pick-me-ups).

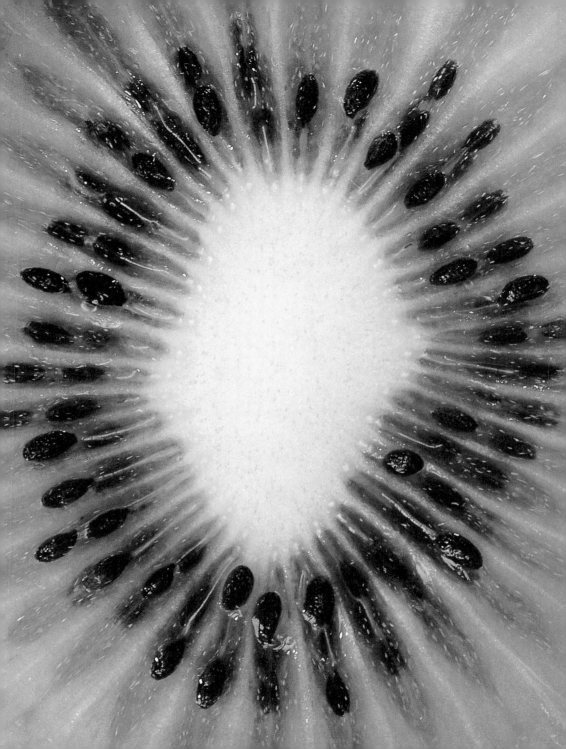

# A few common foods not mentioned so far . . .

You may have noticed that lots of common foods have not been mentioned. Many of these are low in nutrients and actively damage both your health and the environment. We must always consider the health implications before putting anything in our mouths.

**Sugar**

White sugar rots teeth and is extremely high in calories. It has been linked to the recent sharp rise in cases of diabetes and obesity. Carbohydrates and naturally occurring sugars in fruit and dairy produce will provide all the energy requirements for even the most active of teenagers.

Sugar also has an addictive quality. The more you eat, the more you crave. If you do have a high sugar diet (due to fizzy drinks, sweets, puddings and ready meals – which often contain sugar to make them seem more satisfying and tasty), cut down gradually, replacing white sugar with honey (organic or local, not the mass-produced stuff where the bees are fed on white sugar), which is more natural and healthful.

**Margarine**

A lot of people think margarine is better than butter. I beg to differ. It's a highly processed food which turns grey in the manufacturing process. They then dye it yellow to make it look more appetizing – more like butter, in fact. A thin scraping of butter never hurt anyone. Alternatively use oils – which can be flavoured with herbs for variety (see page 61 if you're reading this book backwards or opened this page at random).

**Biscuits, cakes etc.**

High in saturated fats and white sugar, biscuits and cakes fill you up but don't provide nutrients in useful amounts. Unless the packet states "suitable for vegetarians", biscuits may include a fat derived from worms, sucked out of the mud of seabeds. This plays havoc with the ecosystem, since it destroys the natural habitat of many sea creatures as well as denying fish the worms they need to feed off. Added to that, it's a revolting thought, a creamy sugary confection being made of worms. Or you might see it as an apt metaphor. It rather depends on your attitude to biscuits.

**Crisps**

High in fats and salts, crisps make you fat and spotty. In America, crisps are called chips. In Britain chips are what the Americans call fries. Indulge occasionally if you must, but a baked potato is altogether more satisfying and better for you. Also, please note that the packets crisps are sold in are impossible to recycle or reuse, so they're hopeless from an environmental perspective.

If you must have crisps, buy large packets (organic, additive-free) and decant your rations to save on all those bags.

Don't worry about your school being denied books or a computer. There are other ways to raise funds for these. You don't need to collect crisp packets to do it, as is fashionable in the UK. Spread the word.

**Junk food, fast food and take-aways**

The only thing burgers, fried chicken – all that junk – and the obligatory accompanying French fries are good for is increasing the wealth of the companies which sell them. They get richer and we're all the poorer for it. Forests are cut down so that cattle can be raised for little money in order to produce cheap meat. Chickens are bred in appalling conditions, fed rubbish and pumped with hormones. These poor birds are so fat they can't even stand on their legs. But then they're kept in such cramped spaces they have nowhere to walk, anyway.

Like crisp packets, much of the packaging generated from burgers etc. cannot be reused or recycled. It is the cause of major litter problems and adds to the rising mountain of rubbish that has to go somewhere – either into landfill sites or into incinerators which throw up toxins into the atmosphere.

Junk food is low in nutrients and high in salt, artificial flavours and saturated fats. A direct correlation (link) has been found between the rise in obesity and the spread of junk-food outlets.

Much of junk-food advertising and marketing is directed at young people. It can therefore be difficult to comprehend, especially if you've been brought up to believe Jolly Meals are a treat, that such food could really be an evil. That's because they have clever people dreaming up scheme after scheme to persuade you to part with your money and good health.

Be cleverer. Join the growing number of caring individuals, many of them (no)alternatives, who boycott such outlets. There are plenty of right-on options such as wholefood cafes, delicatessens, homemade picnics and home-cooked food.

Our home is a sanctuary. It protects us from "out there". And yet everything is connected. How we behave in our homes influences everyone and everything on our planet. We can choose to make that influence positive, affecting the quality of our air and water and the health of the earth.

Live in your home as you would have others live in theirs: with respect, with love and always with a thought for all our futures.

# Your home and beyond

# The green bedroom

YOU WON'T ALWAYS BE ABLE TO CONTROL WHAT OTHER HOUSEHOLD MEMBERS BUY OR USE AROUND THE HOME. BUT IN YOUR OWN BEDROOM, SURELY, YOU HAVE AUTONOMY. WHEN ADOLESCENCE ARRIVES YOU WILL FIND YOURSELF GAZING UP AT YOUR FLUFFY BUNNY WALLPAPER IN DISGUST AND DOWN AT YOUR KIDDY-ORIENTED BEDDING IN HORROR. "WHY," YOU WILL WONDER, "DID I NOT NOTICE BEFORE? HOW CAN I POSSIBLY BRING FRIENDS IN HERE?"

Time for a mature makeover. Ignore those home-decorating shows which slap on the paint and shore up shed loads (forest loads, more like) of MDF. Follow my tips, go searching for further information in books and on the web and give your bedroom an eco-makeover.

Eco-friendly products might seem expensive, but when you're saving the world, it has to be worth it. You could contribute to costs with money raised through babysitting and other helpful activities. But if you're clever in your choices, an eco-makeover can save you money.

## Furniture

Second-hand furniture is cheap and, if it's old, likely to be better made than modern stuff. You can always paint it with chemical-free paints to match the room's colour scheme.

If you must have new furniture, choose bamboo (the fastest growing totally sustainable wood) or rattan, which is made from vines, one of the nine "woods" considered magical by witches.

A new bed to accommodate your growing limbs could have a bamboo or rattan headboard or be made from reclaimed wood or wood carrying the Forest Stewardship logo (see page 163). That way you know that our ancient forests won't have been ravaged. Use anything else, apart from second-hand, and the guilt could keep you awake at night.

## Curtains and bedding

Natural, organically grown materials are the best. For curtains choose from hessian, cotton or hemp. Bedding can be hemp or cotton. If your funds really won't stretch to organic, consider buying second-hand. Wash your purchases well when you get home and bless them with a spray of lavender water in a pump-action bottle.

Curtain and bedding exchanges are springing up all over the place. It's a bit more expensive than a charity shop, but the quality might be better and you'll have more to choose from.

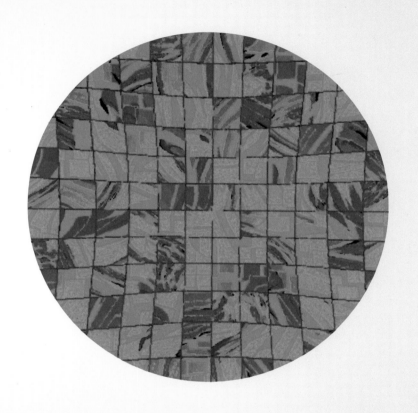

# How to patchwork

Patchwork is an old craft favoured by witches, who hid charms and magical tools in them where the witch hunters wouldn't find them. It's easy to do and it can be constantly expanded. Each piece of cloth, which can be embroidered, tells part of your life story.

One witch in the drop-in coven has a "life quilt" which includes material from her children's first pyjamas and a piece taken from the hem of her wedding dress. Every favourite item since, that she wore until it fell apart, is included. It has great energy. Shop-bought bedding can never match such a unique item.

The ambitious among you might like to try hexagons or other symmetrical shapes. I'd stick to squares. These can be hand- or machine-sewn. Sew squares together to form strips, before joining these together. The bigger the squares, the quicker it grows. For a totally fast duvet cover or curtains, don't bother with squares at all – do stripes.

As well as duvet covers and pillow cases, patchwork can be used for cushion covers and throws to give old furniture a new lease of life.

If you're good at needlework, you can make pillow and duvet covers. My mother used to sew large square patchwork quilt covers using old dresses, often picked up at jumble sales. I even had patchwork curtains at one time. It's a great way to use up old articles of clothing that no one else is likely to want (because they're stained or totally worn through in places) and that would otherwise be sent to the recycling depot.

Old cloth can also be used to recover second-hand cloth-covered lampshades to match your room and maybe pick out certain colours and themes in your patchwork.

If you need a bit of privacy, instead of using net curtains, you could crochet or knit some window covers. Use large needles and they will let plenty of light through while blocking the snooper out. They can easily be fringed with shells and small hag stones or any other crafty bits you have to hand, such as beads or feathers They'll look superb.

## Colour scheme

The four best colours to enhance creativity and pep up the imagination are blue, light green, yellow and white. Black and red are to be avoided, however Goth you might be feeling while looking at paints.

Only use eco-friendly paints, free from health-damaging chemicals. One company in the UK, called Ecos, now produces a paint which soaks up chemicals in the air that have leached from furnishings. How clever is that?

## Carpets

Bare wooden floorboards are fine if you have rugs to warm up the room, and better for asthma sufferers. But avoid this latest craze for wooden tiles unless they have the FSC stamp of approval. Second-hand carpets and rugs are

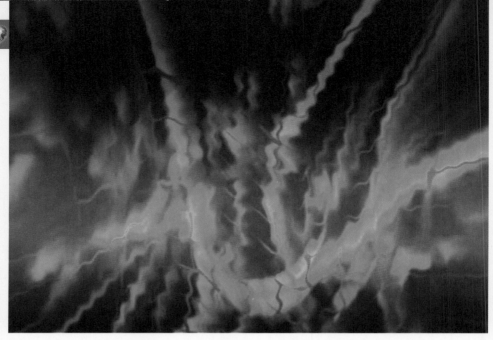

easy to come by. And one last word on patchwork. I had a gorgeous carpet when I was a girl, made from carpet samples, taped together from the underneath. It was so sweet. Some carpet shops will give these samples away when they change their range.

You could also have a go at weaving a rug. Get a couple of long wooden poles and two shorter ones. Build an oblong frame. Loop string around it lengthways so that it looks like a harp. Thread strips of material or bits of wool in and out, using a wide-toothed comb or even your fingers to bunch it tightly together.

Many hands make light work. So leave a basket of strips and wool next to it and guests won't be able to resist having a go. Rag rugs can also be bought quite cheaply. If it's a fair trade product you'll know the makers, often from an impecunious part of the world, have received a fair price for their efforts.

## Hi-Tech stuff

Televisions have no place in bedrooms. If you insist on having one, keep a cloth over it so that it doesn't dominate the room and make sure it is placed more than 2m/6ft away from where you sit, to protect you slightly from radiation. Prolonged exposure to these invisible rays causes allergies (asthma, eczema etc.), immune problems (colds, sore throats etc.) and maybe, in the long term, cancer.

Always keep the TV switched off at the mains when not in use, again to protect you from radiation and to conserve energy. Video recorders and hi-fis should also be switched off at the mains. If you have a computer in your room, keep that switched off too when you're not going back to it for more than an hour. Screensavers might save the screen, but they can use up more energy than when the computer is in use. If you're taking a screen break – 15 minutes within every hour is recommended – leave the room, or you'll still be absorbing radiation.

If you can only afford one energy-efficient light bulb, fix it into the light fitting you use most.

## To spiritually cleanse your space

Light a sage stick and waft it around the room, then ring a bell in each corner.

## Tidying

The best way to keep a room tidy is to divest it of every unnecessary item. If you haven't worn something for over a year, give it away. Look at all your ornaments and knick-knacks. Do you like them? No? Then get them to a charity shop. Still coveting childhood books and toys? If you're not emotionally attached, pass them on to a child. Keep a minimum on display if you must and store the rest for the future. I saved my favourite dolls and teddies for my own children. To keep soft toys free from asthma-causing dust mite, let your cuddlies sleep in the freezer occasionally – this kills the little critters off. Then wash and line dry.

Once you've cleared the clutter, keep it that way. Avoid a consumer frenzy, buying yet more unnecessary stuff just to fill the shelves and satisfy a spending urge. Instead get out and find, for free, natural items for your altar to Asa and Akasha (see page 18).

## Caring for your bedroom and the world

◯ When dusting – if the thought ever occurs to you – a drop of lavender oil or lemon juice on a damp cloth is much better than a wax spray.

◯ Always remove your shoes so that your carpets remain clean and won't need to be vacuumed so often. Nor will you bring outdoor pollution into your sanctuary.

◯ Clean mirrors and windows with one part water to 10 parts vinegar. You can put this in an old pump-action bottle and use newspaper to wipe it off. Brings them up a treat.

◯ If – when – you spill ink on your carpets cover the stain with milk and it will scrub up – you will then need to wash out the milk with a bit of water and washing-up liquid – phosphate-free, biodegradable washing-up liquid, of course. Witches and (no)alternatives favour using ink pens and bottled ink because plastic throwaway pens are an unnecessary waste of resources and don't biodegrade.

◯ If your carpets are dirty, sprinkle them with bicarbonate of soda, leave for half an hour, then vacuum. For extra fragrance, add chopped and crushed herbs, such as rosemary and lavender, to the bicarbonate of soda.

◯ If you spill wax on your carpets, cover with a brown paper bag and smooth over using a medium-heat iron. This will melt the wax, which will then be absorbed into the paper.

# Houseplants

Here's a tip that doesn't have to be confined to the bedroom – it can enhance the whole house. Certain plants are able to purify air tainted by chemicals leaching from modern building and furnishing materials as well as household cleaners. Some can even counteract the effects of cigarette smoke and pollution from nearby busy roads.

The plants recommended have been tested by NASA space scientists, who use them as purifiers on the space shuttle. They found that a spider plant, for example, can absorb 87 per cent of indoor pollution in 24 hours. Magic!

So even if you don't have a garden, you can exercise your green fingers, reaping many of the benefits to be gained from outdoor horticulture and at the same time bring balance and purity to all who breathe within your home. Get the balance of the Elements right for each plant species and it will reward you with health, growth and sometimes, depending on the species, flowers.

That's all there is to it. I have recommended some easy-to-use books at the back of this one.

# The plants you need

There are others, but these are the easiest to grow: spider plant, philodendron, bamboo palm, chrysanthemum, mother-in-law's tongue, ivy and the peace lily.

Just a quick note about chrysanthemums. Some nurserymen spray them with chemicals to stunt their growth. Obtain chyrsanths from a local gardener who I'm sure will be happy to get you started with the gift of a tuber.

## Top Tips for growing indoor plants

○ Arrange plants in groups to provide interesting contrasts and shape. In doing so you can provide shade for sun haters using sun lovers. The plants work together!

○ Always have a dish under pots to catch excess water.

○ Never leave a plant standing in a full drip dish of water for longer than half an hour – it rots the roots.

○ When rinsing alcohol bottles for recycling, add water to the dregs and feed it to your plants – they love it!

○ Covering the soil with crystals, pebbles and shells will keep in moisture so that plants don't need watering so often. It's a practical spell.

○ Plant feeds should be organic.

○ When plants dry out, plunge the pot in a bucket of water and keep it there for 20 minutes.

○ Always soak plants in a bucket of water before potting on.

○ When potting on, cut back dead or dying roots and a little bit of good root to allow easy take up of water.

○ Borrow plant books from libraries. They're free if you return them on time.

○ Check out second-hand shops – they're an excellent source of plant books, old pots and interesting drip trays. Such things need never be bought new.

○ Learn from others – avid houseplant collectors will be happy to share their knowledge. It's always easier to watch than to read. Gardeners will probably give you cuttings, too.

## Plants need

○ sufficient but not too much water

○ either direct sunlight or no direct sunlight, depending on the plant type

○ the right-sized pot for the species and the plant's age

○ annual potting-on (moving to a larger pot) for most but not all plants

○ clean leaves so that they can breathe – so wipe them regularly with a damp cloth

○ regular feeds at certain times of year

## Clear conscience

Clearing our conscience allows us to accept that we're not perfect but gives us the chance to make positive changes to the way we live.

It can apply equally to changing over to the (no)alternative lifestyle and the way you conduct relationships with family and friends, plus any other habits of an unsavoury nature that are best put behind you. As I said in the first chapter of this book, a clear conscience helps you sleep, study and be happy. If your conscience is clear, you have no need of guilt.

## Conscience cleansing spell

**a piece of recycled paper**
**an ink pen and ink**
**a beeswax candle**
**a heat-proof bowl**
**rosemary oil**

On one side of the paper write down three habits you could do without. Then light the candle and breathe according to the instructions on page 30. Say out loud, "The time has come for change, my life I'll rearrange. Out with the bad, in with good, I'll live my life as a good witch should."

You can use a different word to describe your religious belief if you don't consider yourself to be a witch. Alternatively, use the word "person". Take the paper and hold it above the flame, but don't allow it to catch light. As you do so, say, "By this fire my conscience is cleansed. By this fire I make amends."

On the other side of the paper (using both sides of every sheet, halves the amount of paper you'll ever need – think of the trees that'll save), write down three good, new, healthy habits that you can easily welcome into your life. Take as long as you like to decide. Now pass the paper above the flame (but again, don't let it catch light), saying, "By the power of the God and Goddess, by the might of their fire, give me the strength to heed my desire. It is my will and so will it be that I strive for the good of all and for me."

Add a few drops of rosemary oil to the paper and keep it somewhere safe. Each new moon and full moon, take it out and read through the habits you vowed to stop and those you vowed to embrace and ask yourself, "How am I doing?" When you have fully integrated your positive resolutions, and ceased all the negative, do the spell again, casting out another three bad habits and introducing a further three good ones.

The following pages contain plenty of ideas for this spell.

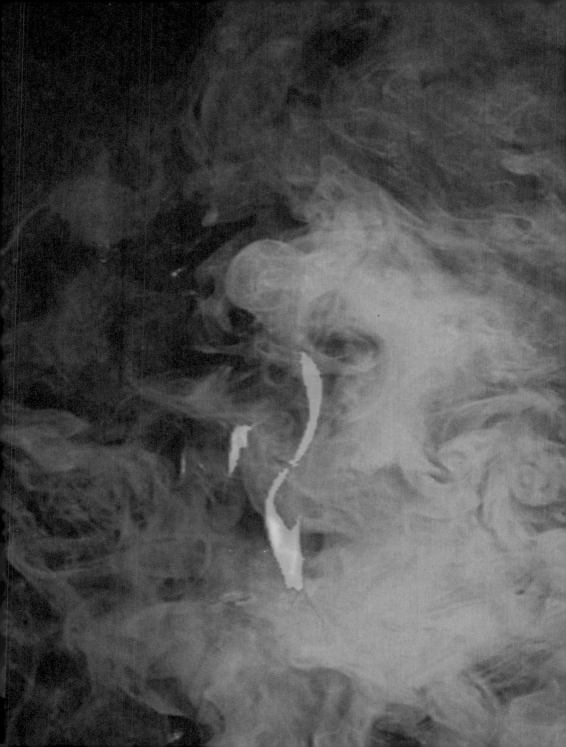

## Save the Elements and Spirit

You may have noticed that lots of the spells use symbols of the Elements and Spirit in the rituals. Witches aren't daft. We know the importance and sacredness of Water, Fire, Earth and Air in the sustaining of life, which is what Spirit is. Whether you consider yourself to be a witch or not, you can still do your bit. It's the only way to save the world and survive.

## Easy-peasy energy-saving Tips

Saving energy in the home is something we can all do. You may think some of the tips a tad dull, but not every world-saving activity involves waving banners and marching on governments. Every little helps and if everyone was this efficient the overall demand for energy from non-renewable resources and nuclear fuel would drop, meaning a cleaner, greener world and a slow-down in global warming.

● Use energy-efficient light bulbs. They cost more than the usual bulbs but they can last up to 12 years (so take them with you when you leave home), which will save you a fortune in the long run.

● In the kitchen, when making hot drinks or preparing herbal rinses etc., boil only as much water as you need. If cooking or heating small amounts, use a small pan on a small ring (or keep the heat low on a bigger ring) and use a saucepan lid.

● Your best dress is in the laundry basket and you want to wear it now. Select any other items in the right colour and wash those as well. If there's only a small pile, use the "half load" setting on the washing machine, or shove it all back in the basket and wash the dress by hand.

● At dusk, draw your curtains and tuck them in behind the radiator if there is one. This will keep the room warmer. So turn down the heat on the radiator while you're at it.

● Further energy may be saved by installing a reflective panel behind radiators on external walls, since it allows heat to be reflected back into the room. The panels are available from DIY stores. If you can't get hold of these, kitchen foil is almost as good. A shelf built above the radiator will also help to keep the heat where you want it (and will be a perfect spot for growing seeds if you keep the soil moist).

● Never leave electrical appliances switched on when you're not using them. Even leaving things like TVs, video recorders and stereo systems on standby wastes a lot of energy so turn them off at the mains. (A whopping 80 per cent of the energy used by video recorders occurs when they're not in use.)

● Before you switch on the TV, ask yourself, "Could I be doing anything more worthwhile instead?" You could read, study or go for a brisk walk. If you end up at a friend's house watching TV, at least you'll only be using half the energy that you would have if you were both sitting

alone at home doing the same thing (so long as your own equipment isn't on standby).

● Buy a Trevor Baylis wind-up radio. This amazing clockwork device works for an hour or longer if you get the model with a solar panel. Then you simply wind it up again (supply details from Freeplay, see page 235).

● Fit draft excluders to windows, doors and mail-boxes. You'll notice an immediate change for the better.

● Turn down the water and central-heating thermostats by one degree (or a bit more if you've sorted radiators and draft excluders). Chances are, no one else will notice the difference, until the bill arrives and it's less than usual – by as much as 10 per cent.

● Feeling cold? Put on an extra jumper and wear slippers. Blankets are also good for snuggling.

● You've heard this one before. Shut the doors between rooms to keep the heat where it is most useful: i.e. your bedroom, a den or living room.

● Avoid using tumble dryers on days when the wind and sun can do the work for free.

● Ask your parents to buy their energy from renewable sources like the European company Unit(e), which derives all its electricity from willow burning, wind and wave power (details page 237).

# Easy-peasy water-saving Tips

It's a funny old world. First we're told sea levels are rising because of global warming. Then we're told we don't have enough water and we have to conserve it. So what's that all about?

Well, the thing is, sea water contains salt. We need fresh water. Because of farming and industrial needs, a few people are hogging all the water, keeping it for themselves. One country will build a dam while another may divert an entire river. This really does happen. Then the people downstream get nothing but a muddy dribble. It's sick. It's the cause of wars!

In the west the amount of water we consume means our rivers can dry up in the summer months. Dry rivers can't support fish and other creatures that need to live and breed in or nearby water. On top of all this, we pollute the waters we do have. Why is such crazy stuff allowed to happen?

However, as long as it is, these are some small but significant ways to help:

● Take more showers and fewer baths. A relaxing soak with essential oils is a welcome treat before exams etc. But you can easily apply your potions with a flannel.

● If you do have a bath, siphon off the water into a butt or straight onto the garden.

● Install a water butt outside your home to collect rainwater which can be used to water your garden.

● Use only eco-friendly products in your bathroom and kitchen. These can be bought from health-food shops and sometimes (I don't know why only sometimes) from supermarkets. They don't cause the algae growth which feeds off the phosphates in things like cleaning products and washing powder. These algae stop sunlight and oxygen reaching the fish. This kills them.

● Don't eat farmed fish. The waste kills the seabed and spreads disease to wild fish. Commonly farmed fish include salmon and trout.

● Install a brick or a device called a hippo in the water cistern of your toilet so that less water is used for a flush. Or install a dual flush system – less water for liquids, more water for solids.

● Wear organic cotton or hemp. See page 150 to find out why. If it's too expensive for your budget buy second-hand clothes, or revamp

those you have. This reduces the need for so much cotton production.

◉ Campaign against the building of dams around the world which, for political reasons and profits, divert water from those who need it. Write to your president, prime minister or state governor – the people who authorize funding for these projects. Tell them their dam(n) policy sucks and will influence the way you vote when you're old enough to do so.

◉ Eat organic food (see page 50).

◉ Use a cup of water to clean your teeth instead of allowing the tap to run.

◉ Celebrate LowTide (see page 223).

◉ Avoid power showers – they use almost as much water as baths.

◉ Wash and dry dishes by hand (at least occasionally). Dishwashers use up a lot of water (and energy) and the steam sends chlorine into the air where it pollutes the atmosphere.

# Easy-peasy air-saving Tips

We need oxygen in order breathe. If it's polluted we can become ill. Pollution also contributes to global warming. Helping to keep our air clean by taking on board the following tips is easy because many are cheaper than not caring.

○ Ride a bicycle or take public transport rather than waiting for your parents to give you a lift all the time.

○ Boycott celebrities and their products. Flying all over the world promoting yourself contributes to global warming. Producing masses of unnecessary branded items encourages consumerism, which is also a major cause of global warming.

○ Plant trees. Five trees will counteract the effect of the $CO_2$ emissions caused by an average family car in the UK every year. So really, it should be five trees for every year your family owns a car. Get digging, or send money to a tree-planting charity.

○ Try to shop local or have food delivered to your home rather than relying on supermarkets all the time. This will improve the stock local shops carry (eventually) and reduce everyone's reliance on supermarkets. This reduces car use.

○ Suggest your parents walk instead of using a car for short journeys. Alternatively, offer to run down the local shops for them.

○ Buy fresh food produce grown locally and in season. This will mean less energy has been expended on growing it in heated polytunnels and glasshouses. It also won't have been flown over in an aeroplane.

○ Avoid flying halfway around the world or across a continent to sit by a pool and read a trashy novel. Instead, travel around the country in which you live, discovering the history of the land and its peoples.

○ Take on board all the energy-saving tips (see page 82). Less burning of fossil fuels means less global warming and pollution.

○ Encourage car pooling. Your parents may know someone living nearby who takes practically the same route to work as they do. If you live in the sticks, there is no school bus and you can't cycle to school, encourage parents to take it in turns to do the school run. This requires communication.

○ If you have younger siblings who are driven to school for safety reasons, ask if a walking bus scheme can begin. This involves youngsters wearing bright tabards and walking together. It's great fun and good exercise for all involved.

○ If you must use a dishwasher (see water-saving tips on page 86), ensure the cleaning products are chlorine-free.

○ Boycott all wood products that don't carry the FSC logo.

# Easy-peasy earth-saving Tips

Our earth is sacred. We need it to grow food. It supports trees that help with the creation of oxygen. It is beautiful. And yet we hack down the trees and pollute the soil. We also have a nasty habit of digging ruddy great holes in it. We fill these holes with rubbish which, by definition, is stuff we don't need. Why have it in the first place?

● Reduce the amount of packaging that comes into your home. Leave excessive packaging behind in the shop and tell them why you are doing so (it's unnecessary and what are you supposed to do with it?).

● Boycott goods altogether if their packaging cannot be recycled and choose a similar product which has packaging that can be recycled or has no packaging at all.

● Refuse plastic bags and tell shopkeepers why (they don't biodegrade, they fill up landfill sites, when they litter the countryside they suffocate and choke animals, in seas they do the same and their use sends the wrong message out into the world). Using non-renewable resources to produce stuff we use once and throw away makes no sense at all. (No)alternatives hate plastic bags.

● Avoid take-aways and home-delivered cooked meals. Too much packaging.

● Reuse everything you can. Wrapping paper can be reused, card is useful for making homemade cards, jars and bottles are good for herb oils (see page 61) and storing bulk-bought kitchen supplies of things like rice. Bulk buying reduces packaging.

● Repair household items rather than throwing them away.

● Recycle whatever can't be refused, reused or repaired.

● Compost uncooked kitchen waste (but not fish or meat).

● Compost garden waste.

● Start a wormery for cooked kitchen waste. They can be tricky until you get used to them, but they are so useful. They help with the waste crisis and produce a great soil for you gardeners. Order one from Wiggly Wigglers (see page 237)

● Never use peat-based compost. When peat is dug up it deprives wildlife of important habitats.

● Encourage friends and family with babies to use washable nappies rather than disposables.

● Eat vegetarian meals.

# Easy-peasy spirit-promoting Tips

Life is more than a heartbeat and breathing. It's an energy, a feeling. When we work towards common goals with others, we feel this Spirit. It creates a sense of belonging and makes us feel happy to be alive. The following are just some of the things you can do to promote Spirit.

○ Grow a wildlife garden at home or at school.

○ Join a campaign to save an endangered species.

○ Join a campaign to save an endangered nation or tribe.

○ Buy fair trade goods which give profits to the workers. Everything from coffee to candles can be fair trade and will be labelled accordingly.

○ Help organize a festival or party to celebrate the natural wonders of our environment.

○ Vote, when you're old enough, for any party that puts the health of our environment and the world's peoples at the top of its agenda. Be wary of liars. Hold them to their promises.

○ Green your school. A representative of a local environmental group such as Friends of the Earth, Greenpeace or the local council may be able to help you. They can audit the school's use of resources and advise how to improve things. Money saved can be spent on something to benefit the pupils and staff.

○ Green your home. Encourage your parents to get involved.

○ Keep notes on wildlife seen in your garden and while out in the countryside. Note when the various plants begin growing in spring. Report your findings to wildlife charities. It helps them to assess the effects of climate change.

○ Help out at a local charity fund-raising event.

○ Discourage the use of slug pellets which harm wildlife. If snails and slugs are eating seedlings and plants, go hunting for them and drop them in a bucket containing an inch of water and a large handful of salt, then wrap them in newspaper and bury them. If you lob them over into a neighbour's garden they will return. They have a homing instinct of around 40 metres/45 yards.

○ Put a bell on your cat so it can't hunt birds and small mammals so successfully.

○ Join a samba band, so that you can help provide a carnival atmosphere to demonstrations, ensuring they remain peaceful. Learn to stilt-walk, too – it's impossible to rampage when you're wobbling about on stilts.

No two families are the same, but most have common threads. The best families are ones where each member is respected for their individuality. At the same time what you have in common is celebrated, promoted and protected.

Look after each other and your home lives will be happier and more harmonious, while your daily lives will become easier to cope with. The key word, as always, is love.

Obviously, we all have moments that we can't claim to be proud of. But do your best and encourage other members of your family – through love and understanding – to do the same.

*Your family*

# Seven steps to a harmonious home

The following family rede applies to every member of the family:

- Share meals together
- Listen
- Avoid rows and the causes of rows
- Lead by example
- Respect privacy and space
- Never lie
- Be reliable

## Family meals

It may be breakfast, lunch, dinner or a late supper. But at least once a day, the whole household should sit down together and eat.

Switch off the television, lay the table and gather round. Families that eat together are always happier families. Too many of us eat at separate times or eat facing the television. Reverse this trend which is damaging not just to individual families but to society as a whole.

## Listening

*Soft of eye, light of touch,*
*speak little, listen much*

Wiccan Rede

Listening is a great skill, essential to the art of conversation. Allowing others to express their views or to get stuff off their chests helps them to relax, feel better and comfortable enough to ask for advice. We all have our reasons for not listening. We might tune out to avoid being told what to do. We might be too busy to stop what we're doing, or too tired. We might feel we have nothing to say in return.

Sometimes we don't converse because we're past talking, fearing the inevitable rows that develop from the most seemingly innocent conversations.

It's easiest to hear each other when the telephone answering machine is on and mobile phones and TVs are switched off.

Once channels of communication are open, talking becomes easier and more things can be discussed at any time.

## To start listening

Light a candle, heat some rosemary or peppermint oil on a burner and say: "We all seem so very distant and far away. Tell me, how was your day…?"

## Avoid rows

Rows never solve disagreements and are damaging to relationships. When we row we say things that we don't mean. Once started, rows are difficult to end. This makes everyone unhappy, including those not involved. Their torture is listening to loved ones shouting abuse at each other.

We row when we feel unable to talk or listen, usually because discussion has failed to resolve certain disagreements.

Rows continue because no one will admit to being wrong, even if deep down they know they're out of order or not wholly right. Instead of saying "sorry" we go on the attack.

Rows also brew through the over-familiarity that comes with living in close proximity for years. Our conversations become devoid of simple words like "please" and "thank you". We fail to show our appreciation to those who do the most for us. If you have been cooked for three times a day for the last 12 years, it's totally possible that you will take such activities for granted.

Plus, if you have been asked to do a particular job umpteen times, you can hardly expect the word "please" to figure in the umptyfirst request, now can you? Or expect a triumphant fanfare of applause when you have completed a long-awaited task.

Another reason people row is that they feel they are being criticized. Any conversation that begins, "You always do this and I hate it" is likely to end in a row. Far better to begin with, "It upsets me when you do this because...."

If all family members follow the seven clauses of the family rede, harmony can be restored.

## Vow not to row

A spell for all the family and a good ice-breaker once you've hugged, made up and dried your tears.

Make a crown of fresh bay leaves – if you don't have your own supply of bay, you may be able to obtain a few sprigs from restaurants, hotels and formal gardens which often display bay trees.

Alternatively, many private homes continue the ancient tradition of planting two trees by the front door. Ask permission before "pruning", and make it a neat job. Give thanks to the Spirit when you have acquired enough for your laurels.

Keep the leaves attached to their twigs and tie them together to make a crown, using white ribbons or thread.

Place the crown on your head and say, "I look to these laurels to bring lasting peace to all who take their turn beneath. What's gone before is now the past and now's the time to love and laugh. We look to the future and shall not rest till rows are done, for that's our quest."

Invite everyone with whom you share your home to take a turn wearing the crown and making the vow.

# Lead by example

Grown-ups aren't always right. It can be a shock to discover this and it may take time getting used to the fact. But telling them boldly that they're wrong about anything, in your opinion, is unlikely to change their minds.

Remember that parents have their own histories, their own regrets, prejudices and upbringing which make them the person they are today. A quick character assassination of your grandparents may explain a lot.

If you are concerned about an aspect of your parents' behaviour or attitudes, whether you consider them racist, unenvironmental or simply selfish, the best plan of action is to lead by example. Be the best person you can be. Be trustworthy, have respect for others, be responsible, be fair, be caring.

Once you have achieved perfection, you will have every right to point out your parents' shortcomings, in a gentle, understanding and respectful manner. But more importantly, if you lead through good example, even the most wayward of parents will follow eventually. For inspiration sit down and watch a feel-good movie like *E.T.* or *Billy Elliot* together and discuss. *Easy Rider* is good, too, for older teenagers. Better still, go walking in beautiful surroundings together. Go out as a family and play.

# Respect privacy and space

Never hog the bathroom at a time when all family members need to get to work or school.

Always ask permission to enter each other's bedrooms and knock first. Never read personal letters, diaries or private paperwork.

Don't play your music really loudly. Whether it's Marilyn Manson or Frank Sinatra, it won't be to everyone's taste at any decibel level. Use headphones or keep the volume low unless you're home alone.

Inviting five friends round to hang out in the kitchen and devour the contents of the fridge every night is tiring for even the most community-spirited of parents. Either take turns going to each other's homes, or cut loose from the gang and hang out with your parents instead. They might not be as "out of touch" as you think. Try them.

Clear up after yourself. Leave the kitchen, bathroom and living spaces how you would wish to find them. What you get up to in your own bedroom is your business, as I'm sure you've told parents. But they're entitled to interfere if they're concerned about fire risks and vermin.

If younger – or older – siblings trash your private space, don't just scream, discuss. Help them to understand how genuinely upset you are. Perhaps a parent can act as referee.

# Never lie

The trouble with lies is that they invariably catch up with us. People who have trusted us find it more difficult if they know we've lied.

Lying for other people is just as unacceptable as lying to cover your own tracks. And friends will ask you to. The usual scenario is that they've lied to their parents about what they're up to and they want you to cover for them. Fine in theory. You're at home, they're out. They get back and nobody's the wiser.

But if your friend's mum smells a rat or just genuinely needs to get hold of her daughter, she'll call you. "Where's my daughter?" she asks. Followed by: "Who's she with?" Good luck.

To avoid such a nightmare, encourage friends to be as honest with their parents as you are with yours. There is no exception to the no lying rule. Even little white lies are unhelpful in the long run. They should be reserved for only the most extreme circumstances when obfuscation (a fantastic word, meaning changing the subject or causing a distraction) has failed. Obfuscation shouldn't fail if you approach enquiries in the right way.

Example: Mother is rather overweight and has a date (well, it's two years since Dad left, so it's about time. It's only because she's been so unhappy that she eats so much chocolate). She's wearing a suit so unflattering that from the back it looks as if she's carrying a sack of bears. "Does my bum look big in this?" she asks.

Do not say, "It sure does, fatso. Time to get your mouth wired." Do say, "I think I prefer you in your green skirt which will still go with that blouse." If she says, "What? You mean I look fat", say, "Not fat, just not as slim as you do in your green skirt." A change of subject is now needed. Ask for a pocket money raise, ask if you can go to an all-night party with your boyfriend. Anything to get her mind right off the subject of her bottom.

You've saved her feelings, you haven't lied (well only a little bit when you used the word "slim") and you know exactly what she thinks about your spending habits, your boyfriend and all-night parties. How's that for a result?

When you're alone together – perhaps when you've just watched her eat an entire chocolate cake in one sitting – this is the time to engage in a tactful conversation about health and diet.

So, are we all agreed? No lying? Good. But not telling lies also involves doing what we say we're going to do, and not doing what we've promised not to do. In short, it's the seventh clause of the family rede: be reliable.

## Be reliable

If your mother says she'll wash your sports kit, she should do it. If you promise to be home by 8.30 p.m., at home by 8.30 p.m. you should be. Give as much warning as possible if your plans change due to circumstances genuinely beyond your control. If you're not going to be home by 8.30 call at 8 to say so, rather than state the obvious at 9.

Feeble excuses must be avoided since they only underline your unreliability. Forgetting is a feeble excuse as you will rightly point out when you discover your sports kit is still dirty. Not having had the time is also inexcusable. Being reliable means being able to manage your time.

# Essential life Tools 4 ✪

## Reliability paraphernalia

You will need change for a telephone and a clock. A mobile phone is seen as the modern equivalent. But you'll still need money for a pay phone if your mobile is lost, stolen, the batteries are flat, you can't get a signal or you're out of credit. Wherever you are, whatever you're doing, change for the phone is essential. It has the potential to save a lot of worry all round – and get you rescued.

If you don't have a mobile, congratulations. They're very bad news for young people. We don't really know yet what harm they are causing, but it is believed that they can lead to brain tumours and interrupt the function of our immune systems. Also, who wants to live near a mobile phone transmitter? Nobody. If they were planning to erect one near your school, I'm sure you'd all, with the encouragement of those living nearby and your parents, speak out against it. You could dress up in bright costumes and paint huge banners with witty messages, some of them in txt spk. You could invite the press – print, radio and TV – and enjoy the jamboree.

But I digress. Now you know how to hold a demonstration, back to clocks. A small alarm clock guarantees you'll always have access to the time. Watches are not the same since they make you a slave to time. Knowledge and slavery are two very different things.

If you are a watch wearer, take it off for a

week and count how many times you glance at your wrist. Not because you desperately need to know what time it is, but out of sheer habit. Time goes more slowly when you're watching. A small wind-up alarm clock means you can set the alarm and relax, knowing it will ring when it's time to head for home, rise early or whatever.

# How To be Treated like a grown-up

When you were a child, it was the responsibility of adults to protect and nurture you. They kept you warm, clean, fed and stimulated.

When adolescence arrives, the dynamics between you and these adults change. Childish things are put aside. You begin to develop adult tastes, you require greater freedom to make choices for yourself and you demand more independence.

As you become more capable and relaxed in the adult world, the relationship between you and the grown-ups develops. You are gradually expected to take some responsibility for your own protection and nurturing. This is the basis of grown-up behaviour, as I explained in the introduction to this book.

When you can prove you are adept at caring for yourself, adults will begin to treat you as an equal, as an adult. In return you must treat them as equals.

Equals do not treat each other like hotel staff. They share the chores. Equals also have regard for each other's personal lives. They look for the underlying causes of grumpiness

and tiredness. Equals do everything in their power to provide help and support.

Sharing and coping together will bring you closer and make others realize just how grown up you are.

To enhance your adult qualities and remove the veil from your parents' eyes that has them seeing you eternally as their baby, try this spell.

# Quite grown-up spell

**a mirror**
**a pentacle**
**a sprig each of rosemary, sage and thyme**
**a beige ribbon – the colour of the universe**

If it's a hand-held mirror, prop it up so that you can see your reflection. Sit cross-legged with the pentacle placed in front of you.

Bind the herbs together, saying, "This sage I bind for wisdom, that I recognize the wise, this rosemary ensures that I remember what is wise. This thyme shall slow my yearning for the passage of time. It shall not fly and nor shall I, from all that I must know, I promise that my soul and mind shall grow as I do grow."

Tie the ribbon and hold the posy to your forehead looking into the mirror. Hold it to your lips, then place it on each point of the five-pointed star, saying, "By Earth and Air, by Water and Fire, by the Essence that holds and works my desire, it is my will and so shall it be that I grow up, soundly with wisdom and ease."

Place the posy near the mirror to remind you that there is much more to being a grown-up than physically growing up.

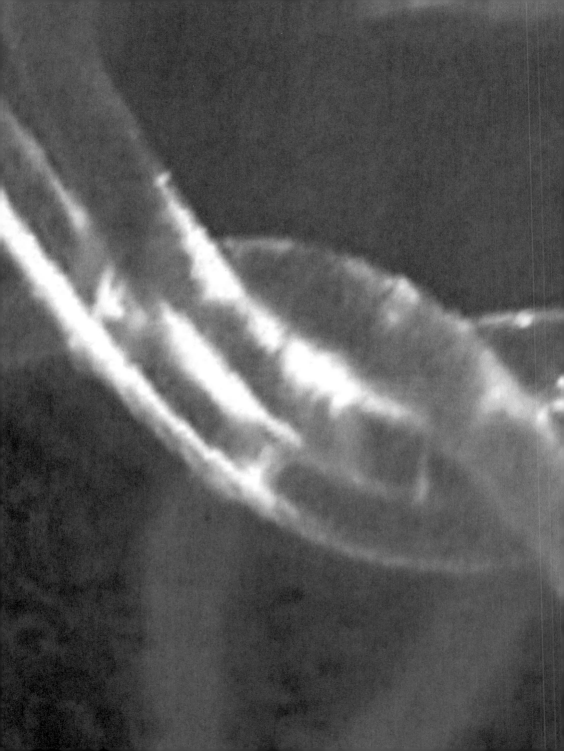

# Divorce part 1: The split

One thing we can always be certain of in life is change. Some is welcome. You'll probably be delighted to leave school, for example. But when your parents announce a parting of the ways your feelings are far more ambivalent.

If they have been married all your life, you will know no other way. The upheaval involved in two people pursuing separate paths after so many years together will affect everyone in the family, even pets. The grown-up leaving will be missed. The parent who is staying may be beside themselves with sadness or other emotions. It all depends on the circumstances of the decision. There may be a third party involved. Or your parents may have drifted apart and now have different interests. Perhaps they can no longer stand the rows and think it's best for everyone if they no longer share the same roof.

Children standing on the sidelines are inevitably hurt, no matter how their parents feel about the situation. Nothing's ever going to be the same again. When we're hurt we can lash out, blaming parents, criticizing them. But we may not know the whole story. Parents may minimize their explanations hoping to save our feelings, or they may be too angry or upset themselves to talk rationally to you.

So you must find it in your heart to give both parents the benefit of the doubt and do your best to support each on their decision. They're still your parents, they still love you. They still care about you. The problem is in the marriage, not with you.

Sometimes the parent who leaves won't be around for a while. This is natural. Don't feel that they are avoiding you. It's the other parent they'd rather not see. Go and find them. They may be feeling as neglected as you. Keep in daily contact by phone if you can and arrange regular meetings.

If there is a third party involved, the parent at home might feel hurt that you want to see their ex. Gently explain that you love both your parents and that you are not prepared to take sides. Give the parent at home equal special attention. Cook them a meal, or treat them in some other way. Maybe you could go out together so that you don't get into a habit of doing exciting things with one and staying in doing boring stuff with the other.

All this requires you to be very grown-up – more grown-up than you might wish to be or feel you can be. Do your best. It's not an easy situation. But in time, it will become easier. Change brings wisdom through experience. This is what builds our character.

I guarantee that by the time you graduate from university, or go to collect an award for outstanding services to your community and the environment, they'll be comfortable enough in each other's company, once more, to share in their pride and joy at having such a well-rounded, beautiful, characterful child. If not, suggest they cast the how to be grown-up spell on page 102.

You, meanwhile, cast this spell. Maybe your parents could show willing and join in.

## Divorce spell

**a locket or small decorated box**
**a lock of hair from every member of the**
**family (plus fur from the pets if you wish)**
**pink thread**
Bind the locks together, saying, "Though we be
parted and broken-hearted, we are one.
Though we be broken, by this token we are
one. For the thread that binds joins hearts and
minds despite this love undone."

Place the hair in the locket or box and keep
it somewhere safe, to treasure all your life and
to serve as a reminder that you are a family
even though you have different destinies.

## Divorce part 2: separate homes

When your parents don't live together you
may divide your time between two homes.
How this is done will depend on the working
and lifestyle patterns of each parent and the
distance between their homes.

Some young people live with one parent in
the week and see the other at weekends.
Others visit a parent only in school holidays
when they have time to make the journey.
Often, in such a case, they stay for longer than
a weekend. This may depend on the parent's
work commitments.

My darling stepdaughter Rosie comes to us
in the longer holidays and her dad travels to
her at other times. She used to visit us every
other weekend, but all the travelling was
affecting her school work. By Monday
mornings she was pooped. So between us all,
including her mother, we made a joint decision

to change the arrangement.

So long as communication channels remain
open – which may involve you acting as go-
between – some sort of plan can usually be
agreed upon. It's far better to sit round a table
than drag these things through a court of law.
If your parents can't quite see this, sit them
down and point out the benefits: less cost, less
hassle and far more mature.

You might find that there are different
benefits to staying in each home. One may be
nearer a place you enjoy visiting. One may
provide a better place for studying. No parent
should expect you to choose one home or
another, as an either/or without any
compromise whatsoever. If they plan to live in
different countries, you're probably better off
staying where you are to complete your
schooling. Visits can then be made during
holidays and the absent parent can come to
see you whenever it's possible.

When your parents embark on new
relationships, which they are entitled to do,
other children may enter the arena. You could
have step-siblings. Or, if either parent decides
to build an extension onto the family, half-
siblings. Be kind and welcoming to these new
arrivals. Babies won't know the story so far –
they think they are the story so far. But older
step-siblings might be carrying lots of
emotional baggage. You can help lighten their
load by listening and doing what you can to
either ignore outbursts or to help them put
such behaviour behind them through kindness
and understanding.

The green-eyed monster, jealousy, can make

anyone of any age act out of character. But, given time and love, such emotions, along with anger, rage and a refusal to acknowledge or deal positively with change, can be overcome.

Try the spells that start on the next page.

## Note to self

An excellent reason not to take sides in a serious parental dispute: many parents work through their mad menopausal moments and then get back together again. We're all entitled to make mistakes, aren't we?

# New sibling Tree spell

a birch tree or other tree suitable for the
climate and position

a small cake, homemade if possible

a drink in a cup

a lock of hair from each of the new
siblings

an old shoe belonging to each of the
new siblings

Arrange with your new siblings to plant a
tree together to commemorate you
becoming members of the same family. A
birch tree is good. Traditionally it is the tree
used for maypoles and the wood burned at
Yule. It is therefore associated with change
and renewal.

These trees do grow tall, so be thoughtful
about where it is placed. In a garden, make
sure it isn't going to cast the entire lawn into
shade. If you don't have a garden, you may be
able to arrange to plant a birch or other tree
as part of a local tree-planting project. You
could even start a local project in aid of Earth
Day (see page 000). Or ask if there's a spare
corner at school. Trees provide welcome shade
on the edge of playing fields.

Take a lock of your own hair and one from
each of your new siblings and if possible an
old shoe each that you've grown out of. Place
these in the hole before the tree is planted. As
you do this, say, "As when the wind blows
from the east, we'll ring the changes, set the
feast. For you blew in just as did I, now let us
greet with smiling eye." Smile and shake
hands. Continue: "By this tree we'll make a
vow to treat each other as family now. That's
me for you and you for me, whatever be our
destiny." Give each other a hug, saying,
"Greetings, brother" or "Greetings, sister", as
appropriate.

When the tree is planted, share the cake
and drink from the same cup. Now look after
one another.

If the other sibling has refused to join in, or
is a baby, share the food and drink with the
grown-ups or leave it as a libation – an
offering. You can still welcome and vow to
look after someone without their mutual co-
operation. Besides, the act of the spell may
well soften them up.

# Home is where the heart is...

**some cloth big enough to make two
  cushion covers**
**red thread and an assortment of old
  beads and sequins (second-hand shops
  are a good source of old necklaces
  which provide plenty of cheap beads)**

Embroider a heart for each member of your
newly extended family with the person's
initials in the middle. Sew the pieces of cloth
together and stuff – old jumpers, past repair,
make good cheap stuffing. You can unravel
the wool, making the cushions softer, if the
jumpers haven't been shrunk into a solid mass.

Decorate with the beads and sequins. The
chant given in the next paragraph can also be
embroidered around the edge or on the back
of each cushion.

As you work, sing or say, "Whene'er we
meet and as we part, we bright the cheeks
and warm the heart. For though we roam
from home to home, when we're together we
share the hearth."

Place a cushion in each of your homes. If
your step-siblings also have two homes, they
may wish to make some cushions as well. That
way, you're all always connected.

# To welcome a new arrival

If your mother or father have a new baby
either with each other or with a different
person, you may be confused about your
feelings. On the one hand you're happy for
everybody. On the other, you may fear you're
being sidelined.

It can certainly feel that way as the grown-
ups struggle to accommodate a new arrival,
who will deprive them of every drop of sleep
and energy. But they're not ignoring you.
They're just suffering from new baby zombie
syndrome. Make them a cup of herbal or
normal tea and help out as best you can
around the home.

If it is a step mum having her first child
with your dad, she may well be over-anxious
with everyone around the baby. If she snaps at
you or is worrying that you could be hurting
the baby in some way, put it down to
tiredness and the natural anxieties that
accompany the early days of motherhood.

Discuss this with your dad, or your own
mum. If it's all a bit tense still in that
department, talk with a grandparent, aunt or
another grown-up you can trust.

Don't for a second imagine a parent's love
for a baby will replace the love once reserved
for you. It's doesn't work that way. When a
new baby arrives it creates more love for you.
A new baby gets grown-ups hormones going.
They feel a great desire to protect and nurture,
not just the little one – there's more than
enough for you and all other siblings as well.

Grown-ups also get all soppy, remembering
the exciting – and tiring – time they had when

you popped out. So be prepared for lots of embarrassing nappy and vomit stories.

See this major change in all your lives as an opportunity to play at being an adult. Take the baby out for walks, try changing its nappy or, when it comes to weaning, feeding it. It will certainly help to focus your mind on contraception when the time comes for you to enjoy the benefits of being a real grown-up.

# Healing

When friends or relatives are sick, they need comfort, sympathy and help. Depending on the severity of their condition and the duration of their illness they may appreciate short visits, with you bringing news of the outside world, or longer stays, where you cook, or potter about cleaning. They might just enjoy the company – it can be very lonely lying in bed.

You must take your lead from them. Respond to their needs rather than assuming this is what they want because that's what Auntie Julie wanted.

Sometimes it's nice to heat essential oils for them. Lavender's always lovely, so long as they don't have an allergy to it (very rare). Or try something like cedarwood which can allay anxiety. Be wary of stimulating oils, though. The patient might need all the sleep they can get. On the other hand they might like a bit of energy – the ill sometimes like to put a positive face on things, however dire the prognosis.

If things are really bad, I recommend frankincense. It gives us a sense of release, making it easier to let go when the time comes. The drop-in coven keeps a bottle in the hospice kit, a special case we use for spells when working with the terminally ill.

It also contains a bottle of thyme oil – public hospitals, rather than private hospices, can be very dirty places. We heat it to kill germs in the air and mix it with water for washing our hands and any bit of the patient that might need it.

When you go to visit sick people, take a bunch of fresh herbs. When you've been

staring at the wall of a hospital ward, a little bit of the outside sure raises the spirits. Even in winter evergreen plants such as rosemary, thyme and sage will be plentiful.

# Bereavement
From me all things proceed and to me they must return.
Doreen Valiente, Charge of the Goddess

On a hillside on the Downs in the south of England stands the chalk figure of the Long Man. He seems to be holding two staffs. Others believe he stands at a doorway. Whichever it is, he is a potent reminder that we come from the earth and to the earth we must return. For this is his positive message.

When our loved ones die it can be frightfully hard to be philosophical. But this is the lesson. We all die. Some believe we come back again. I do. For all natural things on earth naturally recycle themselves. We might come back as the energy in a blooming rose. Our molecules will scatter just as the molecules of countless generations before have and will continue to do so, all things being well. We have eternal life, one way or another. So don't be afraid.

Deal with your anger and your fear and your sense of injustice when you lose a friend, a member of your family or a pet. Do this through meditation and ritual – make a wreath, it really helps – and talk to people who will listen. Listen also to them.

The funeral may be a big affair and you may feel overwhelmed by the ritual. If you can, return to the grave later and conduct a small

# To make a wreath
a **willow ring (a circle of wire or moss-covered wire would be fine)**
**7 sprigs of rosemary**
**7 sprigs of thyme**
**7 sprigs of sage**
**card**
**blue thread**

Attach the herbs to the ring, alternating each herb. Think of the deceased as you do so – what else could you think about?

When it is complete, write on the card, "By this rosemary remember me, by this sage be wise, by this thyme you'll understand how precious are our lives." You don't have to include your name. This is a message from the deceased to the living.

private ritual of your own, one that relates to you, rather than being a hangover from the Victorian era. If the funeral is held at a crematorium, go to a place that has meaning for you and the person who has passed on and conduct your ritual there. When a close friend of mine drowned I made a floating wreath of wild flowers and placed it on the lake. An appropriate ritual for your circumstances will come to you, if you listen to your voice within.

If a death has left you feeling morbid, turn it around into a positive experience by planning your own funeral. Think about what's involved and how you would like to see it done. You could be buried in woodland, with

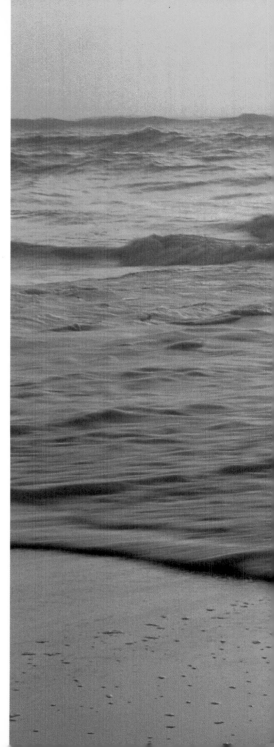

a favourite tree planted above you. You could have a cardboard coffin with rope handles so that no tree needs to be sacrificed. You could have friends do readings and music if you wish. You don't have to have a religious person present, unless those left behind would find comfort in this.

But don't get obsessed with the subject of your own death. Enjoy life. Discuss everything that worries you or you'd like to see done with your parents if you can. You never know, they might think some of these ideas are helpful to them. Chances are, you will all live long happy lives – Elements willing – but there will come a time when you may be arranging a funeral for them. They wouldn't want it the other way around, believe me. To bury a child is the worst grief a parent can know.

When that time comes, make it an honest arrangement with respect for the living and those still to come, as well as a fitting tribute for the person who has passed over to the Summerlands.

Death is a natural progression of life

**M**ore than an instinct, or an emotion, love is a mystical force. It challenges us to know ourselves while changing us at our very core. It sketches out and colours in our destinies.

Like the ocean, which has its calm safe days, love can also storm and rage, wreaking havoc, stirring madness, luring tragedies. Love, like the wind, can waft us gently on a breeze or blow us right off course.

Make no mistake. It's strong stuff, is love. When you're still exploring who you are, taking tentative steps in a grown-up world, while childhood clings like sleep to morning eyes, love can be devilish with its ire.

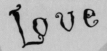

*PLAYING WITH LOVE IS LIKE PLAYING WITH FIRE. UNPREDICTABLE, UNFATHOMABLE. UNIMAGINABLE WHEN YOU STAND OUTSIDE THE LIGHT, UNBEARABLE WHEN YOU STRAY TOO NEAR THE FLAME. LOVE CAN TEAR YOU UP AND PUT YOU BACK TOGETHER AGAIN. AND YOU NEVER KNOW WHEN LOVE MIGHT FADE, OR BE SURPRISED TO FIND IT'S GROWN. ONLY WHEN PASSION DOES SUBSIDE WILL YOU KNOW WHAT FLOWERS YOUR LOVE HAS SOWN. YES, LOVE IS COMPLICATED. WHICH IS WHY IT HAS A CHAPTER TO CALL ITS OWN.*

## Love spells

We don't cast spells on people we love and fancy. Not because they won't work, but because they will. What's the point of going out with someone who's only there because of a binding spell? You'd be better off getting a dog.

Or casting a spell on yourself to increase your emotional wisdom.

## Emotional wisdom spell

**a hazel wand**
**a mirror**
**3 beeswax candles**
**blue paint or an eyeliner**

Draw a pentacle on your forehead. In a dark room light the candles where the flames cannot be seen in the mirror. Hold the wand in both hands. Say, "What is this that fuels my bane, that wroughts my heart with thoughts profane? Be it need or be it greed? Be it of the Wiccan Rede? Come thoughts, speak no lie, bring wisdom forth to know my mind."

Stare into the star via the mirror and listen much.

This spell may also be performed on a beach. You won't need the wand, or the candles, just the mirror and star. Before you begin, meditate on the ideas and myths surrounding mermaids – their power, their persuasion, their danger. But also their beauty, their oneness with their surroundings.

> When the wind blows from the south, love will kiss thee on the mouth
>
> Wiccan Rede

## Here comes the sex bit

When you have met someone special and the time is right, when you adore each other, feel protected, respected and totally in love, having sex is like leaving your bodies to entwine your souls. You think, you feel as one. Have an orgasm then and you'll fly three times round the world (and once round the moon for good measure) before returning to your body. There you'll sink into each other's beings and snooze.

It doesn't happen like that if the boy just wants to get his end away, you're in the back of a car, your parents could be home any moment, you're standing up down a dark alley or you're at all worried or feeling guilty about anything.

My advice is to keep your virginity for as long as possible. Until after you've left home. Until your fledgling adult self is a bit more rounded about the edges and your confidence is sufficient to meet another adult head-on in intimacy. Anyone who says: "If you loved me, you'd have sex with me" is a dork or whatever the new hip word is for a total plonker. Let them go. Turn them into a frog. It's easy.

## Infatuation

Having wild fantasies is natural. You might be busting with lust for your teacher, a friend of your parents, your cousin or a fellow student.

It could be someone you admire, or perhaps they excite you because they come from the wrong side of the tracks.

The thing about fantasies is that everything's ruined when you attempt to make them a reality – the bubble bursts and your feelings go flat.

If you are under age and the object of your desire is a lot older and in a position of responsibility it is essential that you do nothing to express these feelings (other than to a close trusted friend. Often once you let the light in, the desire goes).

Teachers have a duty to their students not to take advantage of them. If a teacher or other adult does respond to your flirtations, chances are you're not his or her first young conquest. You might find it flattering. And so do they. But it is an unequal, illegal partnership, doomed to failure and heartache. It's no way to carry on.

But in the privacy of your own bedroom, alone: "An it harm none, do what ye will."

## To turn someone into a frog

Alone, light some incense or oil, lie back and close your eyes. Imagine them metamorphosing, their mouth getting wider, their eyes bulging, their limbs shortening, until "rivet", they're a frog. Yeuch. Would you kiss that?

# Your perfect partner

There is no such thing as the perfect partner although some are more suitable than others. It may be tempting to choose a partner from your small local pond, but remember that there are seas and oceans out there waiting to be explored. Avoid falling into the trap of having a partner for the sake of having a partner – it causes more heartache than being on your own can ever do.

Choose somebody with a similar level of cleverness to you so that conversation is easy between you. They should be as kind, polite and helpful as you are. They must have a good sense of humour and care about the world. That way, you won't be constantly nagging them about their eco-unawareness, be ashamed of them when they meet your friends or find yourself asking, "What did I ever see in them?"

It is helpful to have a partner who complements your qualities. For example, if you're a fiery, passionate, sun-like woman, you might choose a cool-headed, moon-type man or an earthy green man. Two fiery people together have a tendency to burn each other out. Two cool-headed people, on the other hand, may never even make it to the first kiss.

Some parents prefer their children to date someone of the same religious or ethnic background. There may be plenty of lovely boys or girls to choose from who meet the criteria. But you might have met someone different who is gorgeous all the same. And why not? After all, we live in a cultural melting-pot where the possibilities are endless. If you can, discuss this with your parents before you begin dating anyone. Ask them to explain their feelings, then gently explain why you feel differently. Try not to be too hot-headed, act rashly and live to regret it.

In time you may be in total agreement with your parents for all sorts of reasons. Someone from a similar background can, after all, have plenty in common with you.

Perhaps you can come to some sort of compromise. For example, they may say you can date outsiders, but don't even think about marriage. That's fine for now. Who wants to marry when there's so much excitement ahead, what with further education, choosing a career, travelling and saving the world?

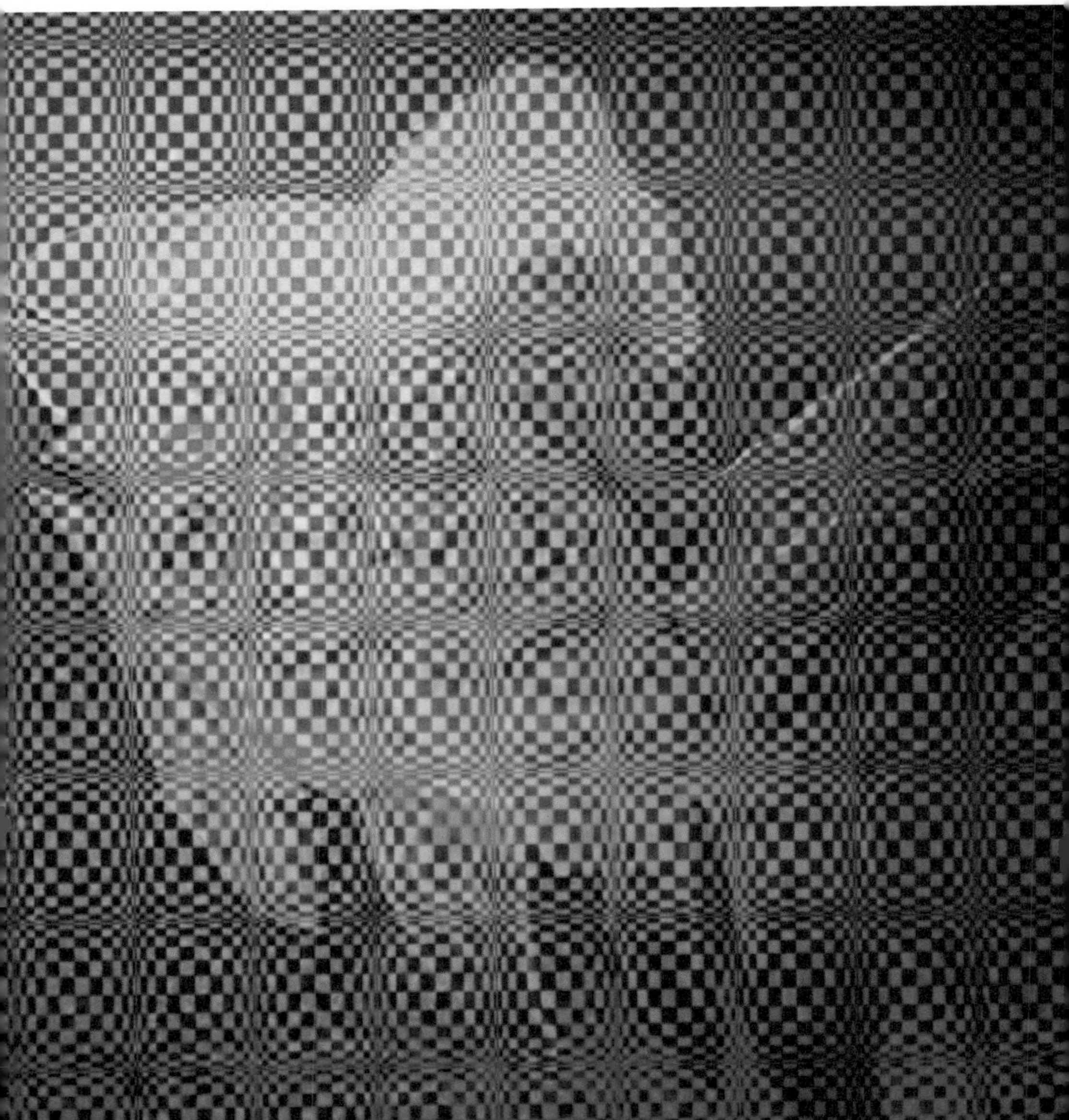

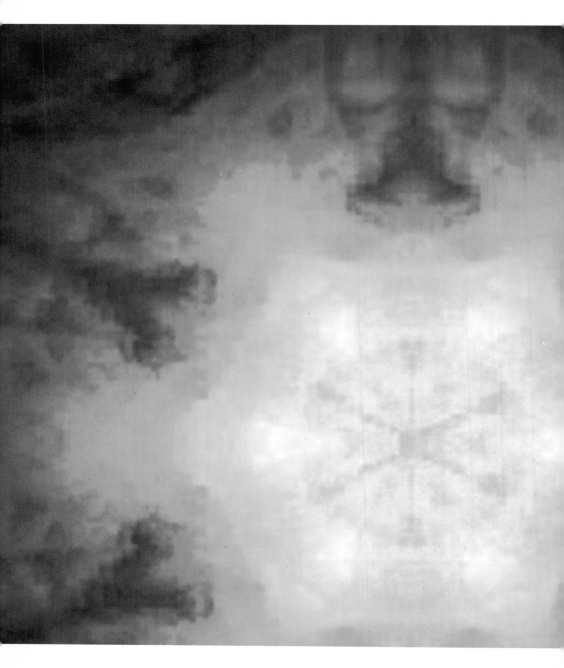

## Courage amulet

Perfect for plucking up courage to ask someone out (or stealing a first kiss).

**a rose quartz**
**pink rose petals**
**a white silk or cotton square cloth**
**a small bowl**

Spread out the cloth. On it sprinkle the petals to form a pentacle (you can draw it out on the cloth first, to make it easier). Place the rose quartz in the centre. Say, "Charged by the Spirit this amulet holds the courage I need to ask my will. Should I be spurned I will be bold, I will find love before I'm old."

Gather up the corners of the cloth, with the petals and stone still on it and hang it somewhere dark and warm for three days. Place the petals and quartz in the bowl. Stir the petals occasionally and repeat the rhyme. Then go for it. Good luck, young witch.

## Dreaming spell
**a bay leaf**

Pop the leaf under your pillow to dream of your future love.

*True in love ever be, lest thy lover's false to thee*

Wiccan Rede

# Be True in love

Wanting to date two people simultaneously suggests an underlying problem with one or both relationships. Never be tempted to date both while you try to work out what's going on. Keeping one relationship running smoothly is difficult enough. Add another to the equation and your life will soon become one big whirl of lies, counter-lies and guilt.

I have a dear friend who says the way a relationship is formed shapes the relationship. If it is one built on deceit, this does not bode well for the future.

Seek out someone you can really trust. I mean really trust. Discuss your conundrum, but don't expect their advice to be perfect. In my experience people tell you what they would do, rather than advise on what's best for you.

If in doubt, put both relationships on hold, then wait to see who you miss the most. You might find you don't need either.

If your partner is unfaithful, finish with them. If, after a suitable duration of penance and repentance, you take them back, be prepared for it to take years for you to rebuild the trust. And don't be surprised if they do it again.

## Note To self

Do say, "You're a lovely person and I know the right girl's out there for you somewhere. But I'm not her."

Don't say, "You're a lousy lover with the personality of a plastic bag. You're dumped, mate."

# If it's all gone wrong...

A time will come when you realize that the best way forward in a relationship is to end it. There is no perfect time to do this. But there are good ways of doing it. Tact and diplomacy help.

If possible cut the cord in the daytime, leaving the person plenty of time to find a shoulder to cry on. Late at night they might cry all the way home alone where their self-confidence is liable to sink quicker than a souffle in a draught.

You might find ending the relationship easier than you thought. He or she might actually have seen it coming and couldn't quite bring themselves to jump first. In which case, it should come as a blessed relief all round.

# Trust in The Wyrd

In the beginning was the Wyrd. It comes from the Northern tradition of paganism, also known as Asatru (meaning true to Asa, the collective name for their Gods and Goddesses). If you are descended from the Vikings – and most of us have a drop of Nordic blood coursing through our veins – your ancestors would have revered the Wyrd.

The Wyrd describes a great web that interconnects all people and events. Whatever you do, whatever happens to you, reverberates on this web. These tremors in turn influence other people and further events. Everything is connected and everything happens for a reason. There is no such thing as coincidence.

When certain things occur, when you meet significant others, you will understand totally the ways of the Wyrd. If you are wise, you will accept that some things are not meant to be. At the same time you will grasp opportunities that come your way.

So, if you are dumped, or the person you fancy hates you, don't worry about it. This was not meant to be. This was not your destiny. I know it hurts. Believe me, I do. I hope this spell helps you to mend.

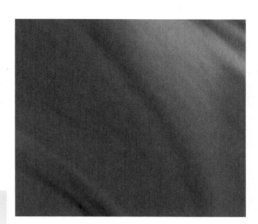

## To mend a broken heart

**a beeswax candle**
**15ml/3 teaspoons sweet almond oil or other carrier oil**
**4 drops lavender oil**
**4 drops from one of the following – choose which best suits your mood**

| | |
|---|---|
| **insecure** | sandalwood or frankincense |
| **angry** | cedarwood or petit grain |
| **despondent** | ylang ylang |
| **lacking confidence** | jasmine (expensive, but you're worth it) |

**Carve the runic sigil Nawt onto the candle about 2.5cm/1in from the top. Run a bath. If you don't have a bath, take a shower. Then mix**

**the 8 drops of essential oils with the carrier oil and massage it into your skin.**

Light the candle (have no other light). Add the oils to the bath, swish them around then climb in. Breathe according to the instructions on page 30.

Close your eyes and imagine a pink light encasing your whole body. Feel the love of the Spirit, and your favourite Goddess and God, surrounding you. Say out loud, "As the fire burns my Nawt fades. As the oils heal, my bane fades. I live by the Wyrd, the Wyrd lives through me. I await the charge of destiny."

Repeat the spell once a week for a full moon cycle. Now enjoy the freedom that comes with being single.

## Note to self

I will use the bath water on plants, indoors or out. I must never pour a whole bath down a plug hole. It's a waste. Marina, who wrote this book, siphons off her spell bath water into butts. She then uses the water when needed on her magical herb and rose gardens. Good woman herself.

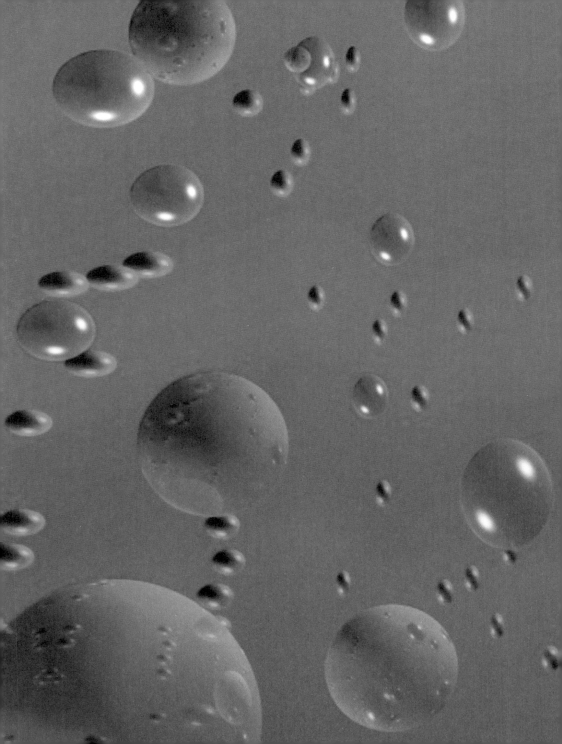

# How To enjoy being single

Yes, I know. Those hormones are raging, your best friend is dating and you want a piece of the action. It's totally understandable. But the anticipation of going steady is often more thrilling than the real thing, because the reality can be so very complicated.

You constantly have to make plans, unmake plans and compromise: "Where shall we meet? When? Please don't be late again. What shall we do? I don't like that film. Oh, all right, but next time I choose. No, I can't tomorrow, I haven't seen my best friend for weeks. I know you don't like her. The day after? But I'm so behind with revision. Sorry, gotta go. Mum's nagging me about being on the phone for so long." And so it goes on.

Whereas, if you are single, you can do what you like when you like. You can choose your friends and the movies you see; you can even wash your hair whenever you like, without having to deal with another person's insecurities. You can also dream or fantasize about anybody without feeling guilty.

In short, being single is an extremely positive state. If you work on your friendships you won't feel lonely. If you love yourself you won't lack self-esteem. As it happens, loneliness and low self-worth are very bad excuses for choosing relationships over singledom. It never works out well.

Far better to make the most of your freedom. Get out into the world and broaden your horizons. The more varied your life the happier and more interesting you will grow to be. And you know what that means…sooner or later somebody just as happy and interesting will find you.

# 10 ideas for the happy singleton

○ Join a club. Every interest from archery to zoology may be catered for in your area. Libraries or your school are the best source of information. Before you know it you could be learning to stilt-walk, playing in a band or winning photography competitions.

○ Volunteer your services to local community groups. If you can sing, why not learn a few old-time songs and visit an old folks' home? If nail varnish or hair braiding is your specialist subject, fêtes and charity events may accommodate your talents by hiring you a pitch or taking a percentage of your earnings. You'll make a mint and maybe some new friends.

○ Get involved in a conservation or gardening group. Fresh air is great for the complexion and the exercise fantastic for the figure. Such activities are also excellent stress-busters. Again, your library will probably be able to point you in the right direction, as may the useful addresses section at the back of this book.

○ Invite your inner circle of friends to an intimate themed dinner party or, when it's warm, a picnic in a park. If you don't have enough friends to form a circle, try the first three suggestions.

○ Go swimming.

○ Get your homework done and dusted on time. Go on, try it.

○ Enjoy a quiet reflective evening in on your own reading up on the lives of Goddesses.

○ Visit an aging relative, preferably one with a good memory, and chart your family tree together. You're bound to get some good family gossip out of it, especially if they have photograph albums. Just look at those awful outfits your parents wore when they were young. No change there then.

○ Ask your mum if she needs any help around the house, but have a chair ready in case she needs to sit down quickly.

○ Cast this spell:
You will need a garland of flowers. Outside, somewhere natural where you won't be disturbed, place the garland on your head and say, "I am one, I am whole, I am ne'er alone. For the world is with me where'er I go. Dance with me world, dance with me now. Let us share the joy of our here and now." Listen out for a tune in the sounds around you and sing along with this chant as you dance. Be warned, this spell may bring you a lover, but only if you truly don't want one. Isn't that always the way?

# The yearn

Not to be too unromantic about it, yearning for a lover is like the feeling you get when you promise yourself you've given up chocolate. You walk past a specialist chocolate shop. The window display is crammed with every delicious variation on your favourite food. You're tempted. But it's closed. How it hurts.

When you're separated from your lover, you don't even have the pleasure of seeing them. If it's a secret lover you can't share your feelings with anybody. You could be in the same room with your lover and you have to act "normal". But all you want to do is throw yourself into their arms and...well, you know. That's the yearn.

But whether it's a secret love, a love kept at bay by strict parents or a separation due to holiday, family or school commitments, the outcome is the same. When you can't hang out together, enjoying being in love, you can only sit and sigh and stare into space, off your food and in no fit state to do anything practical with your time at all. All you can do is yearn.

Try this spell. I find it helps. And it's much cheaper than making long-distance phone calls. It's particularly good if you ask your lover to look out at the moon at the same time. (If you're on opposite sides of the world this is impossible, of course, but the Goddess will hold on to your message until the world spins round.) If your lover is unable or unwilling to be moonstruck, trust in the moon to carry your message of love safely to their heart.

# Yearn spell

**the moon...full if possible**

Raise your arms slowly towards the moon and say, "As one we gaze on Artemis' face and solace comes to ease our pain, for by her presence are we blessed by queenly powers to soothe our bane.

"I send a message now of love to one I miss by the moon above. To my dearest love for whom I yearn I count the days 'til our return. However many moons that be I shall be true to you and me. If it be her will as is it ours our love grows stronger by the hour. And when our hearts do beat as one we'll thank Artemis for all she's done."

You can also send up your own personal message, one that only your lover could understand.

(Artemis is one of many moon Goddesses, a favourite at the drop-in coven. Others include Selene, Luna and Diana. Worship them if you prefer.)

# Out of bounds

You fancy your best friend's boyfriend. You think he likes you, too. What do you do?

You take plenty of cold showers and stop playing gooseberry on their dates. Keep away from him. If that means avoiding your best friend for a while, so be it.

Try talking to him and if the feeling's mutual the conversation is destined to end in a passionate clinch. That will make things really complicated.

## Cooling off spell

**a moonstone**
**5 drops of marjoram oil in 10ml/**
**    2 teaspoons sweet almond or olive oil**
**    in a small bowl**
**a beeswax candle**
**dark purple thread**

Take a cool shower. Tie the thread about 2.5cm/1in from the top of the candle. Say, "I fight with fire this destructive fire. I fan the flames and lust expires. When flame has burned down through the thread all thoughts of (person's name) shall leave my head."

Anoint yourself with the oil. Your forehead, your neck, your chest, your tummy, your thighs and your feet. As you rub the oil into your skin reclaim each part of your body. Make it yours again, and yours alone, saying, "By this oil am I healed."

Pick up the moonstone. Circle it three times above the flame, saying, "I choose to walk my own true path. For that is the way to my own true love."

When the thread is burned through you are free. Carry the stone with you for optimum protection, a reminder of your vow.

In the unlikely event that your best friend's boyfriend is your soul mate, love will eventually conquer all that stands in your way. You will get your man. And lose your best friend.

But it's far more likely that this boy is a bit of a rover. What he's doing to his girlfriend he has probably done to others in the past and will do again in the future.

So take a deep breath and prepare for a spell.

## Note to self

If I snog my best friend's boyfriend, I will find myself caught between the proverbial rock and a hard place: If I tell her what's happened it will break her heart. If I keep it a secret...well, best friends, we don't have secrets, do we?

When the moon rides at her peak, then your heart's desires seek

Wiccan Rede

# Love Token

Handing over something of yours to the one you love says many things: I am yours, we are together, I'm always with you, I'll come back for you, remember me always, be mine.

All of these are quite serious statements, none of which should be undertaken lightly. The swapping or giving of love tokens is a long-lasting tradition still played out in the rites of engagement and marriage in the giving or swapping of rings.

When you choose to give a love token, charge it with this spell.

# Love Token spell

a token such as a necklace, bracelet or
   ring. A lodestone may also be used
   (this magnetic rock has long been
   prized as a love amulet, providing
   courage and determination)
incense
a cup of wine
a pentacle
a candle (in a glass jar to protect from
   the wind, if necessary. Or use a fire)

Outdoors, in bare feet, place each elemental ingredient in a line leaving yourself room to weave in and out between them with no risk of spillage or setting fire to your skirts. As you work think about each Element's associations and how they influence your relationship.

Begin to dance slowly and rhythmically.

Stop first at the pentacle. Circle the token three times above it, saying, "I give of me what I can give, just as the earth does bless with gifts.

At the incense, pass the token three times through the smoke saying, "By the air this shall protect from other suitors and neglect." Over the cup, circle it three times once more and say, "As water's wont to find its way, so shall our love find loving ways." On to the candle. Circle the token three times above it, saying, "By this fire we are as one, this token binds us. Now 'tis done."

See your lover in your mind's eye – or have them with you where you can really see them and say, "By the power of three does my love bless thee, wear this token and think of me."

Your token is now charged. I hope it's appreciated.

# I Think I'm gay

Thinking you are gay, might be gay, could be gay, is perfectly natural during adolescence. As we begin to grow up most of our tastes change, from the friends we like to the music we hate.

Our sexuality is intrinsic to the grown-up we are to become. It's part of the fabric of our personality. It's no wonder we find ourselves exploring avenues that once held no interest for us.

If you think you might be gay, ask yourself why. Is it because you admire a teacher? Have you developed feelings for someone who has been a friend for years? Or have you met someone new?

Often sexuality can be confused with admiration. I'm not saying "You're not gay", I'm just saying that liking someone of the same sex doesn't necessarily mean you are gay. You might be bisexual or you could turn out to be totally straight. Or you could be gay.

If you do think you are definitely gay – because you've talked it through with someone you trust and explored all other possibilities – think long and hard before you come bouncing out of the closet. People can be cruel and ignorant. For some reason they think being gay is wrong. Now, I know it's normal and you know it's normal. But they don't. And unfortunately they get defensive and that's when they can hurt you.

A few people make the mistake of thinking gays want sex with everybody of the same sex all the time. Once outed, deliberately or otherwise, a lesbian may find that no girl wants to sit next to her. A gay boy may find that he's unwelcome in the showers after sports. This is so unnecessary. There's far more to being gay than having sex. It's as much about getting along, sharing common interests, being friends. Just like it is for straight people.

Don't allow prejudices to influence how you live your life. It takes a lot of presence of mind to realize you are gay. However, do be aware

of the law. Just as there are legal age requirements for straight sex, homosexuals are also bound to wait. The age limit varies from state to state and from country to country. Usually it is somewhere between 16 and 21. But in some backwaters homosexuality is illegal at any age.

Generally, these laws have more to do with protecting you than from prohibiting your freedom of expression. Young people may be vulnerable to dirty old perverts of every sexual persuasion. The laws make many of them think twice.

If you are underage and frequenting gay bars, cafes or shops, remember that even if you have sex with someone just a couple of years older than you, they could get themselves into serious trouble. Lying about your age won't always help in their defence because not knowing is never an adequate excuse.

That's the serious chat over with. If you are gay, or think you might be, try this spell. It's not a coming-out spell, it's for helping you realize your true self. Even if you don't think you're at all gay, you might still enjoy the spell, so have a go.

## Note To self
AIDS is a killer. Never have unprotected gay sex or any other kind of sex.

## I Am What I Am spell

an outfit that reflects your true inner self. The clothes should express you and not a stereotypical image. Lesbians don't all dress like men and not all gays dress like women. Far from it, in fact. Therefore, feather boas, false eyelashes and make-up, donkey jackets, high heels or sensible shoes are optional for both genders.

a body scrubber

12 ml/generous 2 teaspoons sweet almond mixed with 3 drops basil oil and 3 drops geranium oil

a copy of Gloria Gaynor's hit single "I Am What I Am"

You may wish to save this spell for when you're home alone. Step into the shower and clean yourself using a natural soap. Get the body scrubber and rub yourself all over, saying, "I call to my God, I call to my Goddess, help me to be, help me express, time to be me, time to be free. It's my right to be the person that's me." Chant as many times as you wish.

Climb out of the shower, pat yourself off with a towel then anoint yourself with the oil. Rub it all over, avoiding sensitive areas. Now it's time to dress. When you're ready put the record/CD/tape on, full blast and dance. You'll soon pick up the words.

# Fertility

The world over, among all manner of customs, superstitions, rituals, deities, sabbats and holidays, there is one resounding and recurring theme: the celebration of fertility.

The survival of any species has always depended on procreation. Fertility has therefore always been something to celebrate and be promoted in order to encourage young people to farm (farming's all about fertility) and to continue the tradition of childbirth and child-rearing.

Because most ancient fertility rites have a "magical" aspect. many academics seem to assume that our predecessors knew little about how babies were made. But I think it's fair to say that our ancestors did know what was involved, because of the stories that accompany the mythology of our Gods. Even the deities created the beast with two backs (old euphemism for sex. Fun, hey?) in order to sire offspring. And when Gods did make babies together, they didn't always support each other. Quite often they swanned off to mate with another – either another God or, in some cases, a mortal. The life of a single mother Goddess can't have been easy.

People not only knew how babies were made, they also knew how to avoid making babies. Read through ancient herbals (books about plants and their effects) and you come across herbs recommended to bring on "courses". Courses is an old word for menstruation. Some of these herbs appear to have prevented conception while others could deal quickly and efficiently with the aftermath if taken in good time. In some ancient tribes from Greece to the Indian Ocean women were even purported to have such strong pelvic floor muscles (ask your mum about those) that they could evacuate semen from their vaginas at will.

Very impressive. But don't try this at home. We spend too much time sitting in chairs instead of squatting, as our foremothers did, to have any hope of replicating this particular form of contraception.

Fortunately, there are plenty of modern methods available to us. And how extremely useful these are. For while children can be a joy, they can also be a burden, severely curtailing the freedoms of women – and girls. And men a bit, but at the end of the day it's the mother who carries most of the load – not sexist, true.

But there comes a time, for many of us, when it feels right to relinquish our barriers and blocks and enter into a union that will bear fruit. There is more to having children than the biological act and the ensuing chaos of nappies, sleepless nights and an extremely curtailed – but generally rewarding – existence. Creating children through a loving union is a spiritual quest that transforms us from a maid to a mother.

As the cycle continues mothers become grandmothers, wise women, what witches call the Crone. I'm currently at the mother stage. If you are a teenager I hope for your sake you are a maid and will remain so for a good many years. As maids you can still celebrate fertility – at sabbats, just as mothers and crones can. But it is always more positive for maids to celebrate fertility when their own is subdued. Meaning, when you finally come to have sex – and sex you will have when it is the right time – enjoy all that you have to give and return as a woman. But take precautions.

If you take no other knowledge or insight away with you from this book, know this: never waste your own fertility by ripening too soon. As a mother I am entitled to say, "You will regret it."

And for those who plan to ignore this advice, taking risks and losing the gamble, can I just add in advance, "Told you so."

If you do find yourself pregnant you will be forced to make a very grown-up decision – without the benefits of growing up first.

You might also – even if you escape fertilization – risk future fertility through contracting diseases which thrive in the close confines of sexual activity and wreak havoc on our tools or reproduction.

## Contraception

The easiest way to avoid conception is to avoid sexual intercourse. But passion has a way of wheedling its way around even the strongest of wills. So have condoms ready when a relationship is suitably established, you are of a suitable age and sex becomes the natural progression of your expression of love.

The withdrawal method (having sexual intercourse and the male removing his penis prior to ejaculation) is not safe – I have two unplanned but very welcome children to prove it.

The pill might be offered, but doctors are unhappy to prescribe it to those of you under the legal age requirement for sex. While the pill is effective it is a terrible water pollutant which may be causing decreased fertility in humans, fish and amphibians. It also offers no protection against diseases.

# Sexually Transmitted Diseases

There are three very valid reasons for avoiding such diseases. Firstly at a time when you are still getting to grips with one of life's great pleasures, your perceptions of sex will be thrown into turmoil. You will find it difficult to trust people, to relax and enjoy something that in the right circumstances can be so special.

Secondly, an STD can endanger your life. Thirdly, it can damage your insides and make it impossible, without the intervention of intrusive fertility treatments, to have children.

To avoid heartache and anguish, get to know someone well before you embark on shared physical contact. Knowing their truthful sexual histories can help you assess the risks, but you still shouldn't have unprotected sex – even if they claim to be a virgin, because you can never be sure they're telling you everything.

If you do have unprotected sex you must visit an STD clinic (a number can be found in your local telephone directory) or make an appointment to see your doctor, even if you don't have any symptoms. This is because many STDs appear to be symptomless. As one STD specialist told me, "We are always delighted to test people and be able to tell them nothing's wrong. There's no such thing as time wasters as far as we are concerned because this is such an important health issue."

You might find the idea of discussing your private parts with a stranger or a family doctor just too embarrassing for words. But you have to be brave, open and honest. It's worth it in the long run. They'll put you at your ease and deal with your predicament in a sensitive manner. The worst (or maybe the best) thing that could happen is that you get a long lecture on the dangers of unprotected sex. Take it on the chin and gratefully accept the gift of free condoms that normally accompanies such chats.

The worst STDs are HIV, chlamydia, gonorrhoea and hepatitis C. None of these displays any symptoms to begin with.

Now I know you probably know all this – there's hardly a shortage of information – but lets just run through the facts to make sure.

## HIV and AIDS

Human immunodeficiency virus, to give it its full name, can only be contracted through unprotected sex or sharing needles with an HIV-positive person. After an incubation period of around 10 years (it could be more, it could be less), most HIV positive people develop AIDS – acquired immune deficiency syndrome. AIDS is always fatal. This is because immunity is suppressed. Without the protection of this natural defence system, AIDS sufferers fall prey to diseases like cancer, pneumonia and, eventually, if they live long enough, dementia.

Those most at risk are homosexual and bisexual men. But an increasing number of heterosexual women are succumbing to this tragic disease that has led to millions of children around the world being orphaned and countless families being torn asunder.

There is growing concern that young people consider HIV and AIDS to be a grown-up, foreign disease that has little to do with them. This is so untrue. Youth is no protection at all. Nor is living in a quiet suburb thousands of miles away from Africa where the disease appears to have evolved and where normal people find themselves attending funerals every week.

If you are at all concerned that you may have been exposed to HIV, you must be tested. This involves having a blood sample taken. You will also be counselled, allowing you to discuss your fears with a sympathetic, highly trained professional counsellor. You should only have to wait hours for the result, but where there is a backlog, you might have to wait weeks. Chances are you will not test positive. But knowing you are okay is better than not knowing either way.

Should you be diagnosed as HIV positive, there are now drugs available that appear to suppress the activity of the virus. Some sufferers, while not cured exactly, seem able to live near normal lives on these drugs, although they are still infectious. Time will tell us how effective these drugs can be in the long term.

HIV and AIDs cannot be contracted through kissing, hugging, shaking hands, sitting on someone's lap or sharing glasses, cutlery, towels or clothing.

# Gonorrhoea

Fact. The most vulnerable group – that is the people most likely to contract gonorrhoea – is teenage girls aged between 16 and 19. This is because the other group most likely to contract gonorrhoea is 24–25-year-old men, who generally sleep with girls younger than themselves. Not only that, but these age groups seem to be living highly promiscuous lives, if not on a daily basis then certainly while on holiday or vacation.

A survey of readers conducted by the popular British "lads" magazine *Loaded*, turned up some horrifying facts. The aim of the survey was to gauge the behaviour of men while away from home. Overall, 44 per cent of men admitted to cheating on their partners. Of these 51per cent were aged between 25 and 34, and 40 per cent were 16–24-year-olds.

Of all those questioned 80 per cent admitted they ignored advice about safe sex and went ahead without condoms.

So don't think you're immune from diseases even if you've been dating the same person for years and have opted to take the pill instead of using condoms.

In both sexes, gonorrhoea can be symptomless in up to 60 per cent of cases, although men will probably have a bit of discharge. Should they notice.

This has serious implications because gonorrhoea provides the perfect environment for the contraction of AIDS. Not only that, but gonorrhoea causes male infertility when the infection spreads to the testes, home of sperm production. In girls, it affects the fallopian tubes where it manifests itself as a pelvic inflammatory disease (PID). The damage caused, even when treated, may be permanent.

A woman who has had a PID is more likely to suffer from ectopic pregnancies (the foetus grows in the fallopian tube instead of in the womb. The foetus dies and so too can the mother. Afterwards, a woman might not be able to get pregnant again by natural means.)

Using condoms during sexual intercourse drastically reduces the risks. But you can catch gonorrhoea in your throat because the disease needs nothing more than a warm wet orifice in which to breed and multiply. So condoms should be used for fellatio (oral sex) as well.

If you are diagnosed with gonorrhoea, sexual partners must be notified so that they can receive treatment.

# Chlamydia

Like gonorrhoea, chlamydia is reaching near-epidemic proportions among young women. Unless you are tested, the first you'll know about your infection is when you fail to conceive – and you could be in your thirties before you try.

In men it attacks the testes and in women, the fallopian tubes. Fortunately it is easily treated with antibiotics. All sexual partners should be notified if you are diagnosed with chlamydia.

# Candidiasis

Commonly known as thrush, candidiasis isn't life-threatening, but it sure is uncomfortable. It's caused by the fungus Candida albicans. Most females have a certain amount of Candida albicans living naturally in their vaginas. It is kept in check by just as naturally occurring bacteria. But if we use antibiotics for any reason, these bacteria may be killed off. The candida is then able to run riot, causing a burning itch, a cottage-cheese style discharge and sometimes pain when urinating.

Men who contract thrush tend to get a swollen head on their penis or an itchy red rash with flaky white patches and peeling skin.

Thrush may also make itself felt when your hormones are imbalanced or when you're stressed or suffering from diabetes. It is easily treated with a pessary (like a pill, only you pop it into your vagina instead of your mouth), which can either be prescribed by a doctor or bought over the counter in chemists.

In the past I've found that a syringeful of live natural yoghurt spurted up inside you can bring relief and balance to the region. Best to do it before bedtime and lie down so that it doesn't spill out.

**M**y life is my party and my body's my temple. That was my motto during my teen years. Parties are covered in the next chapter. This one is dedicated to your body.

If you can imagine your body as a temple you'll be better able to understand its requirements. It must be approached with love and respect and an eye to its upkeep. Ignore its needs and the temple will crumble. Care for your body, worship in it regularly, keep it in good decorative order and with a bit of luck it will last you for years.

# It's your body

# A rite of passage

*STARTING YOUR PERIODS MARKS YOUR TRANSITION FROM CHILDHOOD TO WOMANHOOD. SUCH AN IMPORTANT OCCASION SHOULD BE CELEBRATED WITH A RITUAL.*

The eminent American eco-witch StarHawk recommends a rite whereby a mother and daughter run up a hill together, each holding the end of a red silk cord. When the mother tires, she lets go and her daughter continues to run.

A variation on this theme could involve dancing until the mother tires. Some cultures send the daughter away from the house. When she returns she is welcomed home as a woman with a gift and much ceremony to mark the occasion.

The following is my family's rite. I like it because it tells the story of our ancestry and leaves room for future generations to continue our ongoing narrative. The cord also serves as a reminder of our duty to be good ancestors.

## Rite of passage spell

**A metre/yard or thereabouts of red silk cord rope, or a similar length of hemp rope dyed red with St John's Wort**
**Charms (seashells, locks of hair, hagstones, beads, lockets, odd earrings, rings, talismans, amulets)**

Dying with herbs is a fascinating process. Boil up a huge bunch of herb and add the cord. Leave it outdoors for 24 hours to soak and rinse in salt water to fix the colour.

When it is dried, ask your mother or grandmother to add charms. These should be something of themselves and tell you of their life. They could choose a token of their wedding day or other event(s) that shaped their lives. This will include episodes from your childhood. When your periods begin you are entitled to start telling your own story by adding charms of your own. This echoes your entitlement to live your own life, carving out your own narrative, your own destiny.

The charms should be stitched close together, beginning at one end and placed in chronological order.

When your mother has added what she wishes she passes it to you, saying,

*By this cord the story's made*
*of crone and mother, once the maid.*
*In purest love and purest trust,*
*take heed lest line be turned to dust.*
*When things stand out that must be told*
*stitch it on afore y'are old.*
*And when the next girl comes to now*
*let her continue of our vow:*
*eight words the Wiccan Rede fulfil*
*– an it harm none, do what ye will.*

You may now add a memento of your rite of passage. Not all charms will denote the big life moments such as births, marriages and deaths. You could also add souvenirs from your first Earth Day celebration or LowTide festival (details of these are on page 223). In doing so you remind generations to come that this is what this family does.

When the time comes for your transition from maid to mother wear the cord around your waist to ease your pain and the child's passage into this world, protected by the love of the ancestors.

Invite your eldest daughter to continue this tradition when her periods begin or, if you have no daughters, give it to a son at around the age of 13. And make sure they know the stories and the thought behind each charm.

## Women's Troubles

Painful periods are common in the teen years. Sometimes you get away with a bit of an ache. But if you get a bad one, ooooooch!

Exercise will help, but you probably won't feel like swimming or yoga when you're doubled up with cramps, backache and feeling nauseous.

In extreme cases go and lie down with a hot-water bottle. Or a heated lavender pillow. Wrap it in foil (which can be re-used several times if you're careful) and pop it in the oven for a few minutes. Apply to where it aches.

To make a lavender pillow follow the instructions for a herb pillow on page 61, using lavender only instead of an assortment of herbs.

## Massage cure

Apply this daily when the twinges begin, which may be a few days before your period is due.

**3 drops clary sage essential oil**
**3 drops basil essential oil**
**12ml/generous 2 teaspoons sweet almond oil**

Mix the oils together well. Massage into your lower back around your hips and all over your tummy.

## Herbal Tea help

Alternatively drink melissa or chamomile tea (German chamomile, preferably) with a few drops of lemon juice.

## Sanitary protection

Bio-degradable organic sanitary towels – and tampons can be ordered from Spirit of Nature, a mail order company on the World Wide Web. They're not expensive and can be delivered anywhere in the world. Or invest in a moon cup, the most up-to-date, eco-friendly response to women's natural cycles. Go for it (details on page 236).

Never, ever flush towels or tampons down the toilet. They end up on our beaches. Instead, "bag 'em and bin 'em".

Celebrate proof of your fertility. Don't be ashamed or embarrassed. It's only blood.

# Skin care

It's not fair. One day you're a fresh-faced young beauty without a care in the world. Then – brace yourself – the minute you begin to take an active interest in your appearance and the opposite sex, your youthful complexion – horror of horrors – is obscured with a flurry of spots.

Tempting as it may be to lock yourself in your room and squeeze your blemishes into oblivion, don't. It will only make the situation worse. A simple blackhead, given such attention, might merrily bloom into an acne rash.

How badly behaved your teenage skin decides to be can depend on your genes. Ask your parents, aunties and uncles how they fared as teenagers. Their experience should give you a pretty good idea of what you're up against.

But you can control your dermatological destiny to some extent simply by following the seven skin-care essentials: fresh air, exercise, relaxation, sleep, good food, water and a good cleansing routine.

All but the last of these are discussed on pages 34-40, because they're essential for all aspects of good health. Here's the last piece of your skin-care jigsaw.

# CTM routine

Also known as cleanse, tone and moisturize. You need to do it only in the evenings, to clear away the pollution and debris of the day. This is particularly important if you've been wearing make-up. Leave it on overnight and you have the perfect fertilizer for spots. In the morning, simply rinse your face with water or wipe with a drop or two of Roman chamomile tea – it's good for dry sensitive skins and acne which just about covers everything.

Avoid using soap on your face altogether. Instead, use mild unscented products. It goes without saying that skin products should never have been tested on animals. It will say so on the label. If it doesn't, don't buy it. Look out for symbols from the organizations BUAV, Vegan and Beauty Without Cruelty. These let you know the product is imbued with positive vibes and no bunny risked its sight to test it.

Alternatively, you can make your own preparations. They're good value for money and they work. Plus you won't be gathering lots of plastic packaging that can be difficult to recycle.

First, decide on your skin type.

**Dry** – flaky in places and feels tight after washing.

**Oily** – shiny and prone to acne.

**Combination** – prone to spots and blackheads on the forehead, around the nose and on the chin with flaky or normal patches on the cheek.

**Normal** – may fluctuate between dry and combination, with problems arising just before your period is due.

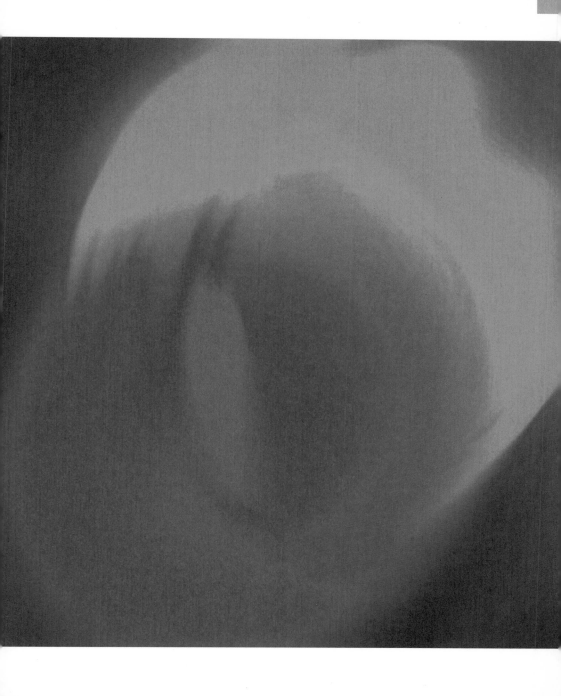

# Cotton wool

I do not recommend the use of cotton wool. Here are just a few reasons why:

◯ Cotton wool is discarded after one use – and it comes in plastic packaging.

◯ Cotton growing is responsible for 25 per cent of all pesticide use in the world.

◯ Cotton farm workers may spend their entire profits on medicine to treat the ailments, some of them fatal, caused by this pesticide use.

◯ The Aral Sea was once the fourth largest lake in the world. In the 1960s the rivers feeding it were diverted for cotton farming. Inhabitants of Aralsk, once a thriving port, can no longer even see the sea which is now 50km/30 miles away. They cannot farm due to salt residues on the land. The trickle of a stream that still runs through Aralsk is contaminated with pesticide and other chemical residues from the cotton industry. There are increasing numbers of cases of anaemia, respiratory diseases, cancer, infant mortality and deformity. Over the doorway of Aralsk's school is a sign saying: "Children are our future." Over to you.

Instead, use a clean face cloth or handkerchief made from organic cotton or hemp. Hemp is a marvellous plant – it can grow anywhere, needs no fertilizer or pesticide and can be used for everything from food to making cloth and beauty products.

Never use cotton wool. Support the hemp industry.

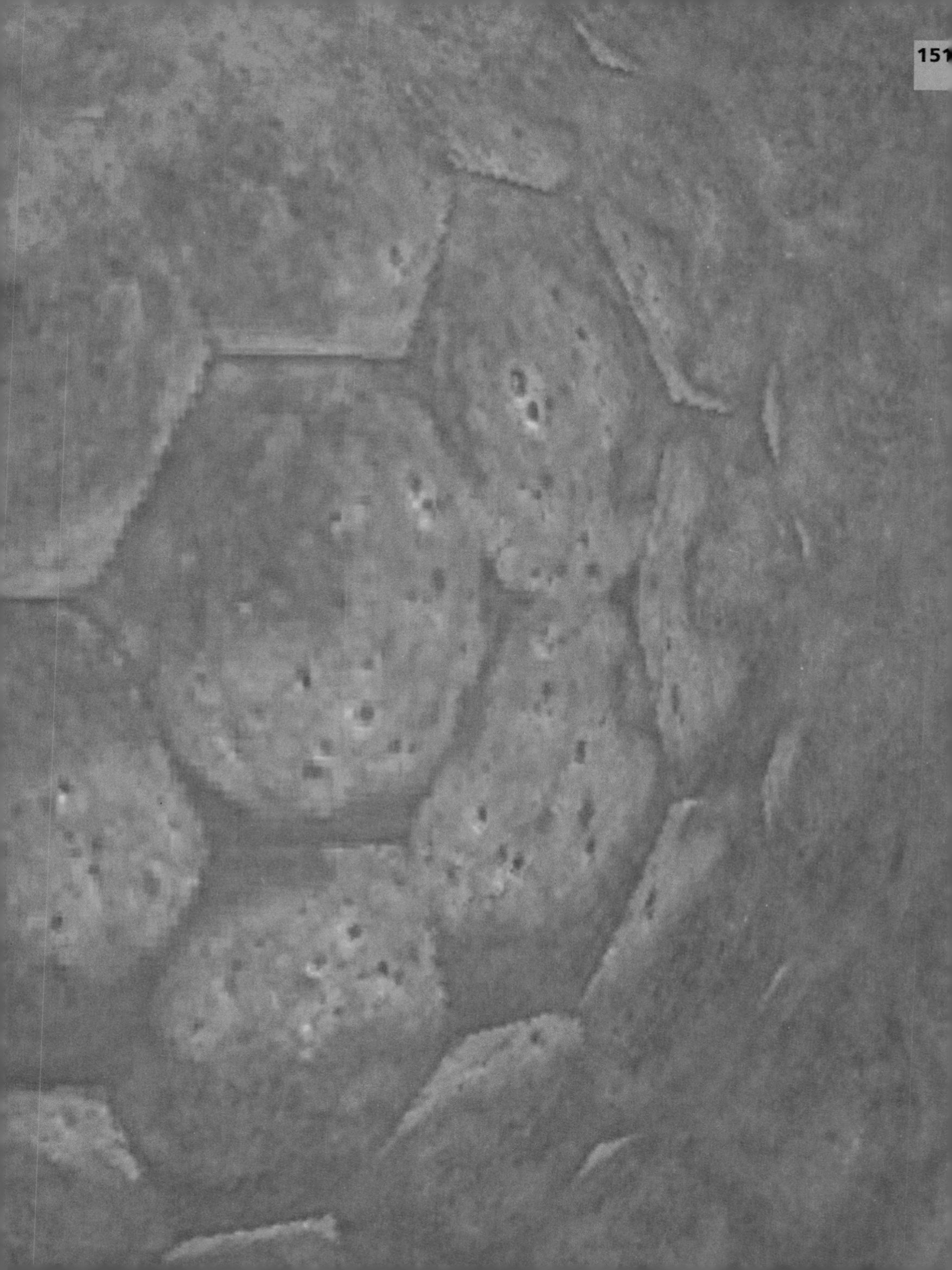

# Cleanser

**dry and combination skin**

10ml/2 teaspoons olive or sweet almond oil or
   unperfumed cleansing milk
3 drops of lavender oil and 2 drops of geranium oil

**oily skin and acne**

10ml/2 teaspoons milk or unperfumed cleansing milk
3 drops of lavender oil and 2 drops of bergamot oil

**normal skin**

Use either the oils or milks mentioned for other skin types
3 drops of lavender and 2 drops of either geranium,
   bergamot or chamomile oil
Mix and apply with a clean damp muslin cloth or flannel
Wipe off with a clean corner of the same cloth and rinse
   face with water

# Toner

**normal and dry skin**

10ml/2 teaspoons strong chamomile tea (1 tea bag
   steeped in half a cup of water for 5 minutes)

**oily and combination skin,
acne**

1 teaspoon cider vinegar
8 teaspoons tepid water
Apply using a clean damp muslin cloth or flannel with
   upward strokes

# Moisturizer

**Dry skin**

5ml/1 teaspoon of unscented moisturizing cream

**Normal or oily skin, acne**

unscented moisturizing lotion (oily skin)

**All skin types**

rose water in a spray bottle. Spray the face with rose water
   and then apply moisturizer with the fingertips using
   gentle circular motions
These creams and lotions can be bought very cheaply.
   Choose a bottle made from glass or recycled plastic (it
   should say on the bottle if this is so )

# Skin Tip

If you have blackheads, try wiping them with a slice of
   tomato or marrow before rinsing with tepid water

# Acne

Acne has to be one of the worst afflictions known to teenagers. Not only do you have to contend with people finding your face off-putting, acne is also painful, comes with a risk of scarring and exacerbates shyness, all of which causes stress.

If you do suffer from acne, know that time is the best healer. But it's little comfort knowing your acne will clear up in your twenties when that's a decade away. Washing with a gentle cleansing agent twice daily using my oily skin formulas will help (see page 152). You could also use the Midsummer face pack (page 154) – but no more than twice a month.

There are plenty of drugs available, such as antibiotics, that will help. There are other options too, such as medicines that dry the skin. These treatments must be prescribed by your doctor who should be happy to discuss your predicament, addressing your emotional as well as your medical needs.

Be strong. Remember, this is a passing phase, albeit a long phase. However low you get over your outward appearance, please understand that it is the inner you that is important, as your friends will no doubt tell you.

Don't allow your acne to drive you into a downward spiral of depression, stress and low self-esteem. For when this happens, your general appearance may slide too. Resist and keep on top of all aspects of personal hygiene. Ensure your hair is always freshly washed, your clothes are clean and keep body odour in check (page 158 might help).

Stand straight and tall, keep smiling and let all who meet you see the twinkle in your eyes as you look directly into theirs.

## Acne away spell

**2 large handfuls of either fine oatmeal or cornstarch**
**up to half a cup of either lemon juice, cider vinegar or milk**
**a small handful of crushed chamomile**
**flowers and a tablespoon of yoghurt may be added occasionally**

Mix ingredients to form a paste, adding a little liquid at a time. Apply the paste to wherever there is acne. Take care to avoid sensitive areas around the lips and eyes. Once the mask is on, lie back with your feet slightly higher than your face and rest for 10 to 15 minutes.

Wipe off with a clean muslin cloth and rinse the face in tepid water. Pat dry.

# Midsummer face feast

Midsummer, a time when the days are long and the nights are short. A time of beach parties, hill side romps, raves, romance and revelry.

Prepare yourself with this beautifying feast of a treatment. Invite friends to join you. And yes, you can lick your fingers.

**a pestle and mortar or a food mixer**
**cucumber slices**
**a selection of the following: strawberries**
**(good freckle fader), peach, water**
**melon, pineapple, banana, cucumber**
**2 teaspoons yoghurt (all skin types)**
**and/or honey (for oily skin) and**
**oatmeal**

Chop and mash your fruits. Scoop a handful into a bowl and mix with your choice of yoghurt, honey and oatmeal. Tie your hair back and smear the mixture onto your face, avoiding the eye area.

Place a cucumber slice over each eye, lie back and relax for around 15 minutes with your feet higher than your head. Wipe off with tissues before rinsing with tepid water.

# Note to self

Clean the kitchen and equipment when finished and check floors and furnishings for drips. Compost the waste from the face mask or leave it out for the birds.

# Hair Care

Some of us let ours grow while others shave it off. And that's just the hair on our heads. During puberty we sprout hair on our armpits and around the genitals. This is perfectly natural stuff. It collects sweat and protects clothing.

But peer pressure and "conventional" attitudes to beauty dictate that this hair be removed. There is no need to bow to such pressure. I don't. If you do choose to remove this hair, opt for waxing which means it won't grow back as quickly as it does when one shaves. Yes, it is painful. So why do it?

If you must shave, use a shaver which only needs the blade replaced. Disposable razors create a lot of waste – that plastic just sits in landfill sites forever.

When it comes to deciding what to do with the hair on your head, your school may have rules determining which colours and styles are deemed acceptable. Try to comply. There's plenty of time for bold bright colours, Mohicans and dreadocks when you leave school. Just remember that your hairstyle makes a statement, so it's helpful to have one that reflects the inner you. However lovely you are, some folk get scared very easily. I once caused an old lady to scream with fright when I was only trying to help her across the road. I'd just been given a skin head by a "friend" (thanks, Chris!) and it scared the lady out of her wits. She thought I was about to mug her.

When caring for your hair, care for others too. Avoid shampoos and dyes that don't carry Beauty Without Cruelty or BUAV logos.

## Hair Treat spell

Make an infusion for your final rinse to
encourage your hair to shine.

**Use 25g/1oz of chamomile (for blondes),
rosemary (for dark hair) or henna
leaves (for red hair).**

Place in heat proof container and pour in
500ml/1 pint of boiling water. Allow to steep
until the water cools. Now add the juice of
half a lemon or a teaspoonful of cider vinegar.
Pour over the hair as a final rinse.

To soften and de-frizz hair, use the same
herbs but add them to olive or sweet almond
oil. Steep for a fortnight, shaking the jar every
day. Apply to your hair and scalp and allow it
to soak in for a few hours or overnight (lay a
towel on your pillow to protect it). Wash
normally and you will feel the difference.

## Personal hygiene

If you suffer from unpleasant body odour, you
will probably be the last to know. We get so
used to our own smell. Your friends should tell
you, but chances are they won't. If you get
given five deodorant sticks for your birthday,
consider this to be a clue.

If your best friend is mature enough to tell
you gently, in private, that you have a
"problem", thank them. Then sort it out. If
you're the friend, be a brick and help your mate.

BO, as young people tend to call it, is nothing
to be ashamed of – it's natural and common,
especially after physical exertion. When we reach
puberty we sweat more. As this sweat comes

into contact with naturally occurring bacteria on
the skin, it begins to whiff.

Avoid smelling by washing your armpits
every morning using a natural lavender soap,
then apply deodorant – purchased from a
healthfood shop to ensure it contains the most
natural, cruelty-free ingredients. Reapply before
exercise or stressful situations.

The following recipes require quite a few
oils. You may have to save up a bit to get
them, but once you have them in your herbal
arsenal they have lots of other uses. See the
aromatherapy list on page 28.

## Deodorizing shower and bath oil
**3 drops clary sage**
**4 drops lavender**
**3 drops juniper**
**10ml/2 teaspoons olive or sunflower oil**

Mix the oils and shake well. There's enough for
two to three doses here. Use sparingly.

Towards the end of a shower, having
washed with your lavender soap, use a
scrubber or flannel to rub the oil on the skin,
giving the armpits plenty of attention. Don't
forget behind the knees and your feet – careful
you don't slip, though. Without the olive or
sunflower oil, this mix can also be added to a
bath, five drops in total.

No amount of armpit washing and
deodorizing will help if you put on a smelly old
shirt or bra afterwards. If clothing is tainted try
the spell on the next page:

## Magic pong-go soaking solution

**7.5ml bergamot (that's three quarters of a standard 10ml bottle of essential oil)**
**5 drops eucalyptus oil**
**2ml/40 drops juniper oil**

Place the oils in a dark bottle with a dropper top. Put the lid on and shake well. In a bucket mix 8 drops with 3 litres/5 pints of water and swish around. Overnight, soak bras, teeshirts, shirts and any other clothing that comes into contact with your armpits before washing them as normal.

If this doesn't work for certain items, they may just be too ingrained. Time to reuse that material. Cut up shirts or vests and use them as kitchen or bathroom cloths or dusters until they fall apart. They can then be composted or taken to a cloth recycling bin. Is there one in your area? Find out. And use it.

## Kissing with confidence

To be enjoyed, kissing needs practice and a fresh breath. Chewing gum's out unless you dispose of it very carefully. Otherwise it can damage people's clothing, choke small animals and birds and make a mess of concrete paving. Avoid it if you can.

If you've been eating strong foods such as garlic or onions, freshen the mouth with a handful of parsley and suck a lemon. Eating an apple also works. Generally if you eat a healthy diet, you won't have a serious breath problem, since this is often related to poor digestion. Meals with much meat, accompanied by alcohol, can lead to halitosis.

Teeth must be cleaned twice daily with a toothpaste made from vegetable derivatives. Toms of Maine and Weleda have good products. I particularly like Toms of Maine, even though they're not a local company for me, because Tom used his profits to set up a community recycling scheme in his town. Good man, Tom.

Avoid fizzy drinks and fruit juices which are high in sugar and acid and can strip the enamel off teeth.

Do not clean your teeth immediately after drinking such things as it will scrub away the enamel further. Instead, neutralize the acid by chewing something like a raw carrot or celery. This encourages the production of saliva which will naturally clean the teeth.

I can't really advise you on how to kiss. If you are connected with the person, kissing always seems to work. If it's not really happening, mentally, the feel of someone else's tongue waggling around in your mouth is rather horrid.

If it doesn't feel right, check out who you're kissing, rather than assume your technique is lacking.

# Body adornment

Stars, spirals, crosses, intricate patterns of
foliage, eyes, fish, wild boar and insects –
they've all been daubed onto the skin, or
wrought of fine metals and attached to the
body or clothing. The belief is that they keep
the bearer from harm and promote positive
attributes such as bravery or wisdom.

Adorning the body (and home) with images to afford protection and enhance positivity is an idea that may well have sprung from the original cauldron of knowledge, so universal is the practice from the Americas to the Antipodes and everywhere in between.

When you choose an image it is likely to have a special meaning for you even if you express this as "I like butterflies. I want a butterfly on my arm." There may well be some underlying fascination with the creature's ability to metamorphose which you can relate to owing to the changes you are currently going through, due to your age and circumstances.

Expressing your feelings artistically is a very good thing. But don't forget that your aspirations and loyalties to certain imagery will change over the years. As will your need to wear your heart on your arm. Some might say, "I'll never change", just as one pop star and his wife claimed before having each other's names etched indelibly onto their flesh for all to see. It took a lot of imagination on the part of the tattooist to change the names into something more emotionally acceptable when they parted company.

For this reason, always choose a form of adornment that will either fade completely with time, such as a henna tattoo, or one that can be washed off with soap, or put back into your jewellery box. Old-fashioned tattoos are too permanent, although there is a new technique that ensures the picture fades over a few months.

# Piercings

It starts with the ears normally. Then it's the belly button, followed by the tongue. Some don't stop until their cheeks, brow and genitals are rattling. Yowser! Too much for me.

And too much for your parents and teachers. Which is probably why you want it done.

If you insist on getting holes punched all over your body, please look after them. Make sure a reputable person conducts the piercings, since dirty needles could infect you with HIV or hepatitis C (as can tattooing).

And keep your holes clean. They stink when they're infected, they look horrible, cause scarring and can make you ill: anyone for blood poisoning? There was a case in America where a girl, following a simple ear piercing, developed a serious infection that was resistant to every antibiotic known to humankind. She lay at death's door for months and is seriously lucky to be alive.

So for a month after the piercing, rinse your new wounds twice daily with four drops of neat pure essential lavender oil or eight drops of thyme oil mixed with warm water. Repeat whenever your holes are looking or smelling dodgy.

# Parent- and self-friendly alternatives

● Celtic knot bangles worn on the upper arm are far easier to remove when you get tired of them than a Celtic knot tattoo .

● Many accessory shops stock stick-on tattoos and clip-on studs and rings.

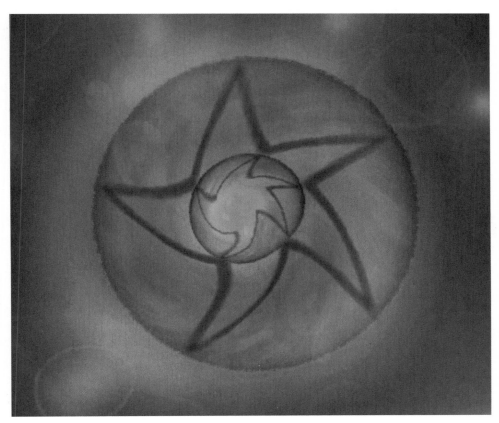

● Wear rings on your fingers and bells on your toes and you really will have music wherever you go.

● Hair slides and braids, ankle bracelets and bindis (stick-on jewels worn in the middle of the forehead) provide an exotic flavour to your look.

● Treat yourself to a professionally applied henna tattoo, which with care (sprinkle liberally with talcum powder and don't wash it) will last a couple of weeks.

● Better still, make stencils, mix up your own henna paste and, with friends, take it in turns to apply. Hindu mates will be good at this – their grandmothers will be even better – since it plays an important part in some Hindu rituals, such as the traditional marriage ceremony.

● Be inspired by the many cultures who paint their face and bodies with natural pigments and herbal pastes. Powder paints might do. View your body as a canvas and express your inner you with patterns and colourful squiggles to match your mood and outfit.

# Symbols for body art and jewellery and some of their meanings

moon — Goddess, magic, feminine strength

sun — God, magic, life, joy, energy

Goddess — moon, wisdom, enlightenment, magic

God — sun, passion, energy, warrior

ankh — an Egyptian symbol of life

cross
(equal length lines) — man and woman, humanity, life

cross
(one line longer than
the other) — Christ, resurrection, worn by Christians for protection
and as a mark of faith

fish — life, water, worn also by Christians as an alternative
to a cross

udjat  an Egyptian symbol for protection

pentacle  the blue star cited in the *Wiccan Rede*. It may represent Venus (goddess of love), Earth or all the Elements and Spirit. A protective symbol for witches, it is also worn as a mark of faith

spiral (widdershins)  rebirth

spiral (deosil)  spirituality

mermaid  the sea, the relationship between humans and the ocean, love, the rocky relationship between lust and love, Aphrodite, divination, knowing thyself. A beautiful symbolic creature – we'll know our seas and oceans are healthy when mermaids return...

CND  Campaign for Nuclear Disarmament – aka Ban the Bomb

FSC © Forest Stewardship Council (this logo on wood denotes a sustainable source. Wearing it promotes the need to respect trees)

# Self-injury

Grown-ups often make cruel comments without thinking. They call us names, insist we could do better at something and criticize our thoughts and habits.

Our brains are a bit like computers. They can be programmed to think anything. Much of this inputting of information is done by the time we're three years old. By our teen years, these ideas have become habitual thoughts. Often we don't even recognize them as thoughts. We interpret them as categorical truth.

When these thoughts contain put-downs, they seriously affect our self-image. Self-hatred, injury and punishment through denial are natural responses to attitudes that we need to unlearn if we are ever to stop hurting ourselves.

You know if you self-harm in any way. What are the thoughts you have when you do so? Ask yourself where these ideas come from. Ask yourself how you can re-programme your brain so that you have a positive rather than a negative response to the thought.

Example: "I'm a nasty little girl." Who says so? Why did they say so? Is it possible they meant, "That was a nasty thing to do"?

Reprogramme. Think, "When I was little, some of my behaviour was deemed nasty. But I'm growing up now and I'm working on being nicer rather than nastier. I'm succeeding."

You might think, "I'm naughty." This thought helped you explain why your parents divorced. But that isn't the case. Tell yourself, "I was called a naughty child. Aren't all young children? But I'm developing self-discipline. It's a shame my parents aren't together. This has nothing to do with my behaviour when I was little. I'm a good person."

To help discover the "logic" that drives you to injure yourself, try scrying. It allows us to look deep within ourselves to interpret how our thoughts influence our behaviour. We are in charge of our own destinies, although luck and karma do seem to influence our paths.

The Etruscans, a people living in what we now call Italy, whose culture predates the Roman Empire, used to scry with chickens. All matters of state were determined by the behaviour of sacred chickens housed in a special temple. Other methods of divination include listening to the rustling sound of leaves (Joan of Arc heard the voice of "God" while sitting under an oak tree), cloud formations, stars, water and mirrors.

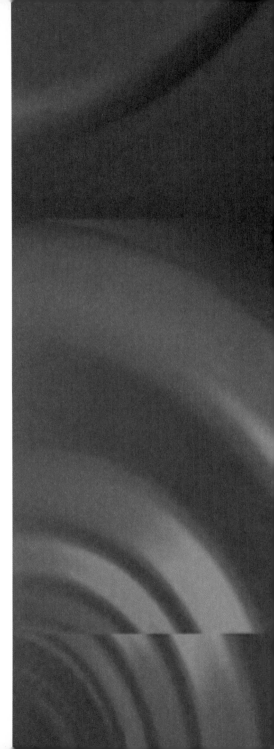

## Scrying spell

For improving self-esteem and encouraging positive thoughts.

**clouds**
**stars**
**a bowl of water coloured with black ink,**
  **or rustling trees**

Lie back comfortably and open your eyes, or ears, depending on your chosen scrying method. If using water, do it at night in darkness save for a candle which you place behind you where it won't be reflected in the water.

Breathe according to the instructions on page 30. Ask yourself, "What is the root cause of my self-hatred? What thoughts tell me that I'm bad or wrong? How can I turn this around to be helpful? How can I sing a more positive song?"

Harmful thoughts may be recognized by the negative language involved. Thoughts tend to begin "I am" and include words like bad, hate, wrong, awful, stupid, fat, silly, naughty, evil, ridiculous, my fault or guilty.

When you find the right thought, hold it there. Now turn it around. Say, "This thought" – then describe it – "is outmoded. It no longer applies to me. I am a wonderful person. That's what I've decided to be."

Write yourself a card outlining your positive new approach. Keep it by a mirror you use every day and speak your words out loud, daily, as a mantra, until the thought becomes one of habit. There's nothing so habit-forming as habit. Indulge in some positive ones, you wonderful person, you.

**N**ever assume grown-ups are right. Indeed, it is often helpful to assume they're wrong. And yet we still have to live by their rules most of the time. Still, if we're teenagers, we should be getting lots more chances to make decisions for ourselves. We won't always make the right decisions. But that's okay. These "mistakes" are what teach us – if we learn from them.

It's Your Life

The following spells and advice should help you avoid obvious mistakes, cope with a few more and explore the potential for creating humdingers — mistakes that can't be put right too easily. Look, no one says life is easy. But it is your life. Grab it and live it and learn.

## Shopping and money

Money money money money money. It's so desirable when you haven't got it. Every advert on TV or in a glossy magazine is torture. If only we could all have those lovely things – those clothes, that jewellery, that right-on-cool-dude bedroom furniture, a pony, a jetset lifestyle, a palace to call home.

I haven't yet perfected my endless supplies of cash spell. If I had, you'd know about it. I'd be that lady on telly who bought the rainforests at the going rate (how much would it be worth as illegally logged timber? Right, here's a cheque. Now go away and take your chainsaws with you.) I would then "donate" the forest to the tribes and animals who already live there.

I'd buy Alaska, as well. It's been sold before. The Russians offloaded it to America when they were strapped for cash. If I owned it, oil companies would never be allowed to drill in the unspoiled wilderness.

Since I'd have endless money I could also throw a fraction of it at a kerbside recycling project in my neighbourhood. We could sure do with one. I'd buy a wind farm as well and give the energy out for free. And pay off the third world debt. That would show those bankers. Dream, dream, dream…

That's the trouble with money. Unless we have absolutely oodles, there's not much we can do with it except survive and spend what little we have on what we can afford.

Very few of us can afford a pony or a palace, a rainforest, wilderness or wind farm. Instead, we buy a T-shirt and nail varnish.

There is a certain buzz that comes with handing over our money in a shop. It gives us a high. It makes us feel empowered, in control. It's like a drug high. An illusion that feels real at the time.

Here are a few spells and tips that might not bring in millions. But they should attract money and make existing resources go further.

# Money~finding spell

There's a bit of a rider hanging on this spell. It works, but only if your intentions are to spend it on saving some aspect of our natural world. The cash that comes might not buy you a mountain but it may stretch to a local Agenda 21 project (see Glossary, page 228) or an event to highlight the plight of something that has captured your imagination.

**a hagstone (that's a stone with a natural hole in it. You occasionally find them on beaches). If you don't have a beach handy ask a witch to help you – they collect them with a passion since each is a gift from the goddess.**
**a green ribbon**
**Air**
**Water**
**Earth**
**Fire**
**Spirit**

Take the stone to a hill top and allow the wind to blow through the hole. Say, "Blood would be easy to squeeze from this, but it's money I need. Air, grant me my wish."

Take the stone to a river, sea or ocean. Repeat the chant replacing the word Water for Air. Allow water to pass through the hole.

Next take the stone to an ancient woodland (this could all take time. But you will enjoy the adventure and the various locations don't all need to be visited in one day). Hug a tree (cos they're lovely things to hug and you might as well, while you're there, and it may bring

wisdom) and appeal to Earth in the chant. Pass soil through the hole as you do

Now you need a fire. I would suggest it contain the nine sacred woods of the witch. These vary from country to country and from coven to coven. At the drop-in coven we consider the nine sacred woods to be birch, oak, hazel, rowan, hawthorn, willow, apple, vine and fir. Nine twigs from nine different trees, that's all you need. Any nine different species will do. Find them lying on the ground rather than tearing them off a tree.

Light the fire somewhere safe, such as a firepit or hearth (please don't accidentally set fire to ancient woodland – this would not help our cause).

Pass the stone over the flames, allowing smoke to pass through the hole. Repeat the wish using the word Fire.

Now wear the stone or carry it with you. When it feels right, give it to someone. This person might be a government official in a mahogany-lined office or a wise Druid in the Red Lion at Avebury (the only pub in England within a stone circle). You'll know when the time and person is right. (It's a witch thing. This is how we operate.)

Tell them, "Blood would be easy to squeeze from this but it's money I need. Can you grant me my wish?" Then explain why you need the cash. The person might not have huge bundles of notes on them, but they should be able to tell you where to go.

If any of you have better suggestions for funding environmental projects I would love to hear from you. Please write to me c/o my publishers.

# Money~stretching spell

When money is too tight to mention cast this spell.

**5 gold coins**
**an earthenware bowl**
**a green bag**
**a new moon**
**a full moon**
**a homeless person**
**a local charity**
**a school**
**a rich person**
**earth**

Place the coins in an earthenware bowl and put it outside overnight at the new moon. The following day store the coins in the bag. Over the next fortnight, before the moon waxes full, give four of them away: one each to the homeless person, the local charity, a school fund (all schools are always fund-raising for something: ask the Parent Teachers Association). The fourth coin should be given to the richest person you know. Implore them to accept it.

The fifth coin you bury during the hour prior to the full moon.

As you bury it, say, "May the seeds sown, grow and grow, and stretch this wealth as far as it may go."

By the next full moon you should see improvements in your spending power.

# Easy~peasy money~stretching Tips

✻ **Buy from second-hand shops**. Such shops are to teenagers what Christmas is to turkeys: an unhappy combination. But you can find bargains if you look closely and have a bit of imagination.

Last year's trouser fashion could be this year's shorts if you just cut off the bottoms. (No? Doesn't appeal?)

Skirt lines can be altered if you're a whizz with the old sewing machine. (What do you mean, what's a sewing machine?)

Change the buttons on that cardie, add a bit of lace and it will be gorgeous. We don't know for definite that some old lady died in it.

Yep, I'm sure you and your mother have the same conversations I have with my step-daughter. But as I say to Rosie (and my mother used to say to me), "It's only a suggestion."

Well, the clothes might not do it for you, but there's usually some suitable material for making patchwork items, such as cloth bags which you could sell to raise cash for new clothes (if you must).

Second-hand shops are also excellent sources of cookery books, gardening books and sometimes crockery. It is very trendy to have a selection of different plates, bowls and mugs, rather than a matching set, which is sooooooo last century. You can often find top-quality pieces which cost a fortune brand new, but are sold for practically zilch in charity shops.

There might also be stuff for spells, such as candlestick holders, plus incense and oil burners. Second-hand shopping is the most eco-friendly, sustainable form of consumerism. Many second-hand shops use their profits to support local hospices and other important charitable organizations. Support them. Witches do.

### ✽ At local shops and supermarkets

Check out food that has to be sold that day – towards the evening it is often marked down in price. This can be an excellent way to pick up organic bargains.

### ✽ Sales

Don't go. If you can't resist, try this spell:

## A spell at the mall

When hanging out at the shopping mall, however much money you have available, budget yourself to half of that. When you feel compelled to buy something, ask yourself, "What is this for? What is my need? Is this going to be useful or nurture a greed?" Don't buy it and move on.

When you've been to every shop, go back and purchase whatever it was that appealed to need rather than greed.

You now have something useful and at least half your money left over for your next session of retail therapy. Result!

### ✽ Carry a citrine

Abundance is said to be attracted to a small polished citrine stone. Carry it in your purse. Your loose change won't want to leave and money from afar will come and join it. If you can't find a citrine, try an amethyst.

### ✽ Join a Lets or Time Dollar scheme

Members of such projects are given a cheque book. You bank credits by doing favours for other members of the

scheme. These credits are spent when you receive favours in return.

Every Lets scheme welcomes teenagers with open arms, because you have unique energies, time, interests and abilities that every community is crying out for. If you joined a Lets scheme you could babysit, walk dogs, go shopping, "sell" herbs, and clean or water plants while folk are away. You could also exercise your limitless creative talents. There are bound to be locals who would appreciate your homemade cards, herbal oils or wine-cork notice-boards with driftwood frames.

In return you'll have plenty of credits to spend on hairdressers, reflexologists, organic home-grown vegetables and plants or practical help with things like painting your bedroom and dress alterations (*someone* will know how to use a sewing machine). Lets schemes are limited only by the skills and resources of those involved.

In one scheme, operating on a housing estate in Hillingdon, England, teenagers do favours in return for vouchers which buy them coffee and Internet time in a local cyber cafe. The rewards on offer through many Lets schemes can "buy" more value than cash earned with a part-time job. For example, two hours' babysitting wouldn't cover the cost of a new hairstyle at a salon, but it could be enough to buy the time of a Lets scheme hairdresser.

If there isn't a favours scheme in your area contact the relevant organizations (details page 236) and start one of your own among friends in your community.

# A~maze~ing problem solver

Mazes are maps which reveal a path to within and without. It's like winding through trees, imagery we associate with fairy- and folk-tales. Mazes lead you around obstacles and to the heart of the matter.

Mazes have been used as meditative tools, serving humankind for thousands of years. They may be carved in stone or created by causing ripples in a smooth pool of water. Some are built with plants.

With the maze on this page, run your finger along its path until you reach the centre, then return to the outside. As you do so, ruminate on a particular problem you're experiencing. You may find that the issue gradually emerges from the dark entangled forest of your mind. In a clearing your problem can now be viewed from all sides.

You will now need a pen and paper to devise a venn diagram. (A venn diagram, as used in maths, helps us isolate issues and join those that are connected. It's all about creating sets.) In the middle of the page write one word to signify the crux of the matter. Around it jot down other obstacles, difficulties and predicaments that stand between you and happiness.

Now draw circles to join problems that are connected. If they stand alone, give them a circle of their own. Give each circle or set a name, such as "This is what I want", "This is what I can't have", "This is impossible", "This has to stop", or "This isn't really my problem". You may find that your problem splits up into school issues and love issues that may be connected to home and parent issues that may or may not be connected to either.

Take one set or circle at a time and return to the maze. Ask the right questions and answers will come. Now act upon them. This may mean discussing issues, changing your habits or casting a spell. At least you now know what you're up against. Rather than one large clump of a muddle, you have bite-sized issues that can be dealt with and ticked off a list. Yes, you're right. That is the difficult part. That's why they're called problems.

# A~maze~ing wishing spell

On a sandy beach, using pebbles and shells or, if the sand is damp, just a stick, draw out a maze large enough for people to be able to walk to the centre. Before entering, pick up a pebble or shell. When you get to the centre make a wish – preferably for the sea. But you could focus on your own problems if you feel they're worse than water's current crisis. Unlikely as that would be.

# Exams

Rotten things, exams. I hope these spells help.

## Revision spell

**a realistic revision timetable which you
can stick to**
**notes summarizing the key issues and
facts for each topic in every subject**
**enough time to write these notes – which
means starting well in advance of
examination dates**
**sympathetic teachers, parents, siblings
and friends**
**determination to do your best**
**confidence that you can succeed**
**nerves of steel**
**several pens that work**

Begin by assessing how many hours you can
realistically dedicate to revision. Take into
consideration time needed for family meals,
relaxation, exercise, travelling, sleeping,
washing, hobbies, chores, day-to-day
homework and occasional spells.

Don't aim too high. If you set yourself
too hard a task you are destined to fall short
of your targets. This leads to guilt and low
self-esteem.

Once you have worked out how much time
you have, decide which subjects need most
attention. There's a touch of the "how long is
a piece of string" to this. You could
concentrate on the subjects you're good at
and enjoy. But that could be detrimental to
your "weaker" subjects.

If you dedicate too much time to these,
your good subjects might suffer. Devise a
compromise. Give your best subjects what they
need, but don't ignore those that require
nurturing. Teachers can guide you in your
appraisal of what's required. And should be
happy to do so.

Now consider when you are likely to do
your best work. I always rose at dawn to
revise. My head was clear, it was peaceful and
I was able to take in masses of information. I
reserved my evenings for socializing, relaxing,
etc., knowing I'd completed my revision
objectives hours ago. Smug? Me? Well it
worked. If you're a night person, however, you
may find that the evening is the most
productive time for studying.

Once you have your timetable organized you
can begin to use it to create revision notes.

At the prescribed hour, according to your
timetable, switch off the TV. In a calm, quiet
environment, sit comfortably and breathe as
described on page 30. Say, "I have the power
to succeed. This power lives in me. It keeps me
calm, it makes me strong, it knows what's
right and shuns what's wrong. I have the
power, I shall succeed. I'll do my best, so must
it be."

Begin to compile your notes. If done
correctly they will aid your understanding of
the subject and help you to memorize the
important points. Take your time. The act of
note-making is as useful as the notes
themselves. Use your classroom notes, relevant
textbooks and, if you can, read further afield.

This gives you access to information that others won't have, which means your work will stand out.

Imagine you are marking a pile of papers, each one regurgitating the same old lessons. Then out of the dirge comes a piece of writing that shines with an unusual depth of understanding. Wouldn't you give it a well-deserved higher mark?

Of course, in maths there is only one right answer. But in English, geography, history, biology, languages and lots of other subjects there is plenty of scope for going the extra mile to provide an interesting read for the (very probably) bored person doing the marking.

USE LARGE HEADINGS. There should be plenty of underlining of salient points. Write key words in CAPITAL LETTERS. Use short sentences to summarize. Develop a code using different coloured inks. Red for absolutely bottom-line facts without which you're bound to fail. Blue could be your general colour. Black might be reserved for personal footnotes, your opinions which show off your broad understanding. Turquoise might be useful for jotting down the page numbers in various books that give more details. You decide what colours work for you.

If using real ink pens, as a good witch should, don't forget there's a Magic Memory Ink recipe on page 182.

When completed, these notes might look brief, but what counts is the amount of work you have put into producing them. If you're not sure whether your notes are ready, ask yourself, "Do I understand my notes?" Does each fact remind you of other facts? Good. Your notes are ready. And so are you.

Enjoy the fruits of your labour.

# Exam Technique

Exam technique requires practice. Teachers will supply you with old papers. See if you can answer the questions within the set time limit.

Practice runs require the same thought as the real thing. Here's what you do:

Give yourself the chance to do well. Always read the exam paper through from beginning to end. Make sure you understand all the questions and the instructions.

How many questions do you need to answer? That question lurking at the bottom – turn the page to see if it continues. Do you need to answer all the questions or choose just a few? Is there one or more section that is compulsory?

Taking time to read through the paper properly saves time and tears in the long run. Anyone who begins scribbling furiously just minutes into the exam isn't likely to get the best marks.

Once you have established what's required, use scrap paper to plan your answers. Jot down relevant points, facts, dates and quotations that you think would be useful in answering a particular question.

This planning really helps. It gives you something to follow should you panic, especially towards the end of an exam when every second counts and you're getting tired. Should this happen, take a deep breath, return to the notes you made at the beginning of the exam and copy them out, adding as much detail as time allows.

Essay plans also let you know if you have enough information to do a question justice. If you draw a blank at the planning stage, this may not be the question for you. Move on. Choose another. The question that seems the most hopeless-looking at first glance might not be so bad if you mull it over for a couple of minutes.

Remember to write your name clearly on every piece of paper. Include any examination codes required. Make sure each question is clearly identified. Never assume the person marking the paper will psychically know which question you're answering. They might be able to work it out, but they'll be miffed at having to bother and may penalize you for their efforts.

You may be instructed to rule off part of the page to allow space for the marker's comments etc. Make sure you do this if asked.

If you must answer every question, when you get stuck, move on. Sometimes the tricky answers bubble up from your unconscious while you're working on easier questions. So you might be able to fill in the gaps towards the end of the exam. If you have time to spare at the end it's always worth guessing – you never know, you might be right.

Keep your handwriting as neat as possible, be careful to use correct grammar and watch your spelling. If you're allowed a dictionary in the exam, use it. There's no excuse for misspelling if you have permission to look up awkward words. Sloppy spelling could lose you valuable marks.

Leave a few minutes at the end to read through your answers, correcting errors and adding the odd additional fact that springs to mind.

Never cheat. If you're caught you will receive an automatic "fail" for that exam and maybe all of them. Cheating doesn't help on any level. Doing well in exams involves exercising your brain, which is useful for keeping it fit and preparing you for excellence in adult life. (It's not the facts that need to stay with you, it's the culture of self-discipline, coping with stress and doing your best.)

That's the technical side of exam technique covered. Now try these spells to enhance your frame of mind.

# Complementary examination spells

## Magic memory ink

The perfect potion for all your study requirements, magic memory ink is guaranteed to keep your mind receptive to normally elusive facts and figures. Use it for revision and exams.

**½ cup of roughly chopped rosemary**
**½ cup of water**
**a bottle of ink**
**a small saucepan with a lid**
**a funnel**

Place the water and rosemary in the saucepan and bring to the boil on a high heat. Place the lid on the saucepan, lower the heat and simmer for 10 minutes to half an hour. After about 15 minutes keep checking to make sure it doesn't boil dry. If it seems to be evaporating too fast, lower the heat or add a little more water.

When the liquid becomes dark and opaque, remove from heat and allow it to cool. Strain the mixture and add to the ink bottle using the funnel (you may have to remove some ink first).

## Note to self

Messing about with ink can be a messy business. I will place newspaper on surfaces to protect them from stains and wear gloves.

## Essential primer

When revising, dab one small drop of rosemary oil on your wrist pulse point and rub with the other. Do the same immediately prior to exams.

If you develop a stress headache, a drop of essential lavender oil can be dabbed on your temples.

## The night before

If you want to read through your revision notes, do so. But this is not the time for ingesting new facts unless you really are on top of your subject and simply want to add a few glorious touches.

The best thing to do the night before an exam is relax. Go for a walk or take part in some other form of exercise to ensure a good night's rest.

Eat a meal high in omega-3, a kind of vitamin that aids concentration. Oily fish is high in omega-3 (if you eat fish). Vegetarians might like to try a spinach and green bean salad with roasted seeds and a hemp-seed oil dressing.

Treat yourself to a bath. A total of five drops of Roman chamomile and ylang ylang oil (three of one, two of the other, you choose which way round) is a good blend for such an occasion.

With the bathroom door shut, drip the oils into the bath, swish it around and wait for a couple of minutes before slipping into the warm comfort of the water.

Get to bed nice and early. If you can't sleep, go flying (see page 38).

## The morning arrives

Eat a good breakfast – see suggestions on page 62. Drink peppermint tea – it invigorates the brain and calms the stomach. Do a few stretching exercises and take a shower. Make sure you have everything you need for the exam – pencils, pens, tools, etc.

Leave plenty of time to get to the exam. If you have time, cast this spell.

## Herbal amulet

**3 sprigs of rosemary**
**a sprig of thyme**
**green and yellow ribbons or thread**
**2–3 drops thyme oil and 2–3 drops of**
**    basil oil (to make a total of 5 – you**
**    choose how you blend)**

Heat the oils in a burner. Sit cross-legged on the floor and begin your breathing (see page 30). When you are calm and relaxed but also quite alert, take up the herbs and bind them into a nosegay, saying, "By these herbs I give my word that I shall do my best. I shall stay calm, with even breath, and seize this day with ease. But should I falter from this course I ask that I be blessed with courage and great wisdom from my favourite deities."

Carry the posy with you throughout the day. Keep it on your desk if that is permissible. If you are allowed to have it out, feel free to squeeze and sniff for added inspiration from the Gods.

Don't forget to blow out your tealight candle before you leave the house.

## Moments before

Keep calm. Breathing as you do before spells will help to keep panic at bay. Breathe and take a ride inside. Away from the throng sit quietly: feel and listen to your breath. Consciously try to slow your heartbeat. Whenever you feel panic arising, concentrate on your breathing. You can and will get through this.

## Afterwards

Avoid discussing your answers, it only makes you feel awful. The exam is behind you. There's nothing you can do to change the result. Oh, all right, there might be. Try this spell. But unless you attend an enlightened academic establishment run by druids or a coven of witches, hang on until you have some privacy rather than cast it outside the examination hall.

## Success spell

**a beeswax candle**
**1 drop of patchouli oil**
**1 drop of myrrh oil**
**1 drop of benzoin oil**

Rub your candle with a warm damp cloth. Mix the oils – a success blend – and rub all over the candle.

Light the candle, breathe (see page 30) and say, "May I be blessed with exam success." Visualize the examiner giving you top marks. See it clearly in your mind. Allow the candle to burn and the visualization to continue for a few minutes before snuffing it out. As you do so, say, "By the power of God and Goddess, if it be your will, so will it be. Blessed be."

Do this at the same time every night for seven days, ending seven days after the last exam.

This spell may be used for different successes. Substitute the word exam for something suitable relating to a job interview or to winning a place at the university, college or school of your choice.

## Note to self

While this spell may be used in conjunction with others, it is not a substitute for the revision spell.

## Results Time

Whether delighted at your grades or a tad disappointed, take time out from your celebrations to give thanks to God and Goddess. Draw a pentacle on the ground. As you work, say, "Spirit, Air, Fire, Water, Earth, bear witness to my grateful praise – to God and Goddess most divine who when I called came to my aid. You gave me strength, you made me wise. For all your help I'm much obliged."

If your results are disappointing, don't let yourself believe for a moment that your future is doomed. You can either resit or vow to do better in future exams.

Teachers and parents may well express disappointment. But what matters is that you gave it your best. Not everybody can be academically brilliant and there are plenty of people in the world who were no great shakes at school but who have since proven themselves to be major contributors to society.

Focus on your successes and think about career options and courses that will allow you to utilize your talents. And don't let your parents compare you with your siblings or other students. Some parents will never be happy unless their child scores grade As across the board. Really, it is their problem, not yours. They want you to be simply super because it makes them look good, justifies the school fees – or makes up for their poor performances when they were struggling at school.

You can be brilliant, you can shine. Just not at exams. Let it go.

# Careers

You will at some point be expected to sit down and discuss your plans for the future. There's plenty of valuable work to choose from. We always need more nurses, doctors, teachers and other heroes to join the emergency services.

You might prefer accountancy or banking, or want to train to be a vet. Whatever you wish to be is your choice. It depends on what makes you happy and where your skills lie.

Before you make firm decisions it's worth taking a year out before university (the gap year) or prior to settling down into a job. Do something outside of your own interests – you might have talents that have yet to be expressed and recognized.

If you live in a city, why not move out to a rural area? The country can offer a very different way of life. It has a slower pace, there's more space, you get to know a broader range of people of all ages. In cities we tend to mix with our own. In small communities everybody counts.

You will also develop a greater understanding of the seasons and have to deal with all sorts of issues that are hidden in the metropolis, such as waste disposal, public transport infrastructures, food production and the effects of climate change. Experience like this is essential whether you plan a career in politics or want to hone your medical or engineering skills in a developing country.

If you already live in the countryside, you may wish to head for the bright lights. But whatever choices you make, insist to yourself that you work for a company that is compassionate towards people and our environment. This makes any job or career more rewarding. If you work for a different sort of company your Spirit may shrivel as you try to juxtapose your knowledge of the real world with the exploitative activities of an organization motivated only by profits. Just say no.

To get a flavour of the (no)alternative lifestyle, join the Woodcraft Folk or an affiliated organization or ask to do some work experience within an environmental charity. Alternatively, contact Worldwide Workers on Organic Farms (Wwoof), which provides information on organic farms all over the world where you can work in return for bed and board. It won't be a holiday. More the chance of a lifetime. Some farms take families, so if you're not yet school-leaving age persuade your parents to dust off their wellies and accompany you. Wwoof and the Woodcraft Folk details are on page 237.

# A spell for sporting success

The power of sporting "superstition" cannot be underestimated, since to be top of your class involves more than physical fitness. You must be blessed with the will to succeed, the determination to come first. This extra magical element is what sorts Gold from also-rans.

Ask your average champion what gives them the edge and they may well describe rituals and amulets. It might be lucky socks, magic trainers, special necklaces or certain rites that must always be performed prior to going out into the arena.

Even if you're not aiming to be a sports star – we can't all be good at everything – rites can help us do better. We might not break a world record but we can beat our own record.

Rites are safer than amulets and mascots for the simple reason that you will always be able to perform them, whereas amulets and mascots can be lost or stolen.

So draw a pentacle in the air or on your shoes and say a short incantation – and believe it. I feel that the words must come from you. It's not difficult. Your spell should rhyme and it should draw on your personal beliefs. Speak to your God or Gods and if you speak true, they may well assist you. If it doesn't seem to be working, train harder.

# Loneliness

Moving to a new school is tough. You may not have been the most popular pupil at your last school, but you had friends. Suddenly you're surrounded by cliques and close buddies and no one makes any effort to include you. In fact they seem to go out of their way to ignore you.

If a new girl or boy enters your class, make them welcome. Sit with them at meals, ask them about themselves and why they moved. Be gentle. Listen. Be trustworthy, loyal. Help them to acclimatize. You might not end up as best friends, but by being friendly you will help them to find their feet and their people. Extend the hand of friendship.

If you are the new girl or boy, you know what I'm talking about. So speak to your mother and cast this spell together. Mums, even if witchcraft is not your thing, do this for your child. It will help them to be happy and to fulfil their potential.

If your mother is unavailable for any reason, try big sisters, aunties, grandmas, dad or any grown-up who knows you well and is willing to help. May I take this opportunity to thank all the mums who have written to me on the subject of their child's loneliness. You are most caring people. Blessed be.

**mum or a suitable alternative**
**a natural place of calm and beauty, such**
  **as a beach, mountain, woodland,**
  **forest or meadow**

Using shells, pebbles, twigs, leaves, flower petals or whatever's available, make a circle together, big enough for you to stand and walk around in.

With your arm out (you could use a wand here), walk round just inside the circle, in a clockwise (anti-clockwise in the southern hemisphere) direction, three times.

Sit down, close your eyes and imagine you are surrounded by a circle of protective light, a force.

Mum, who remains outside the circle, now asks you what you like about yourself. If you can't think of anything, she will be able to prompt you. Go on, all the fantastic things that make you so special. Call them out.

Now think about the others in your class. Describe those you like, including their name, and say what you like about them.

When you have exhausted the possibilities, promise yourself to make an extra special effort to talk to these pupils when you're next in class.

The pebbles, twigs or whatever you used may now be cast out. Throw them into the sea, into a stream or into the air. This is symbolic of your positive qualities flying out into the world where they can be noticed by others.

At school, when you're about to be overcome by shyness or somebody is mean to you, recreate the protective circle in your mind.

## Loneliness dissolving Tips

• Organize car sharing on the school run. This will get you talking to somebody living close by.

• Invite the girl or boy you like most round to tea.

• Get your parents to invite them out on a day trip to somewhere so exciting they can't refuse.

• Parents can join the PTA where they can make new friends who may well have kids of a similar age.

• Volunteer to help out at all school fund-raising events. Pupils will have to talk to you, even if it's only to ask, "How much?" All conversations must start somewhere.

With a fool no season spend
lest ye be counted as his friend
Wiccan Rede

# The dark forces of bullying

Bullies are emotionally flawed individuals. They lack self-esteem and find that hurting others, either mentally or physically, scratches some personal itch of self-loathing. Seeing others pained lessens their own pain. It empowers them – a feeling that is otherwise denied to them. You could pity bullies if it wasn't for the abject misery and harm they heap on others.

Combat bullying every which way you can. Show no fear. Bullies thrive on fear. Without it they are powerless. Stand united against bullies with friends and stick up for the victims. Cast protection, warding and binding spells as appropriate and tell adults in authority about the bullying.

Be brave, young witches. Stamping out this miserable activity is an important task. Left unchecked, a bully will carry on their misery-making into adulthood, where it's much harder and more dangerous to stop them.

## Anti~bully Talisman

Create this talisman working alone or with like-minded friends. You could also work with victims. Each person will need their own stone. If working in a group change "I" to "we", "me" to "us" and "my" to "our" in the chant.

**a carnelian stone if you are a victim of bullying, or a tiger's eye if you are an about-to-get-active bystander**
**a candle**
**a pentacle**
**a small bowl of water**
**incense**

Place the incense, candle, water and pentacle inside the circle. The incense is placed due east, the candle due south, the water due west and the pentacle due north.

Begin at the incense. Pass the crystal through the smoke, saying, "I call to the east and to the air that I might know what I might dare."

Move southwards and pass the crystal over the flame, saying,"I call to the south and to the fire to flame the will for my desire."

Go now to the water, saying,"I call to the west and to the rain, give me the courage to banish this bane."

Lastly to the north, pass the stone over the pentacle, saying,"Yet by the north and by the earth, grant the wisdom of silence's worth."

When working in a group you can chant this next bit together. Hold your stone and say, "This stone empowered by the four watchtowers, protect and aid my Wiccan powers. I act as only a true witch should, never to harm, only for good. But those who would have evil done, by own foul deeds shall be undone. It is my will and so 'twill be, by the cardinal signs and the power of three."

Carry the stone with you at all times. When the bullies set about their bullying, be prepared to stand up to them, but know too when to remain silent for your own protection. They get a gleam in their eye. Their fists tighten or they look for something to throw. Shut up. And run.

## Casting out the clique

Teachers and parents are often oblivious to the cruelty meted out by cliques. They think it's just a group of friends – invariably girls – who hang out together.

Those standing just outside the seeming sacred circle of sisters see cliques for what they really are: a callous collaboration of vain bullies. Clique members single out individuals who are different in some way. They attack with a similar mentality to a bunch of demented chickens pecking on the scruffy hen, the sick hen or the hen who is actually much more interesting and talented than the rest of the flock in some way.

Those most at risk from clique victimization include new girls, pretty girls, clever girls, witches, girls of a different race, less able girls and anyone with problems at home which makes them quiet and sensitive and prone to crying easily – a reaction cliques thrive on.

# To cast out a clique

I love this spell. It has a wickedness about it. Not too wicked, of course. But there is an element of fighting fire with fire. Most gratifying.

**a cauldron or saucepan**
**4 sprigs of rue**
**a teaspoonful of ground black pepper**
**a teaspoonful of ground coriander seeds**
**a crushed clove of garlic**
**500ml/1 pint water**
**something of the clique's ringleader – a**
**   hair, a nail clipping or a small piece of**
**   paper with their name written on it.**

Before writing to me to ask where you can buy rue, try the herb specialists in your area or mail-order herb companies.

Place all the ingredients bar one sprig of rue in the saucepan or cauldron and bring to the boil. When it is boiling, turn down the heat so that the water simmers. Stir in a clockwise direction, chanting, "I brew this potion to protect me, not to hurt the ones who grieve me. By this rue there'll be regret, though, by anyone with bad intent. So. As these seeds sprang from their purses, now we see the clique disperses. Gone is their power, gone by the hour, when the rue and herbs are made to shower."

Decant the potion into a jar or container with a tightly fitting lid. Wash the saucepan or cauldron.

Go to where the clique will be (but not when they're there). Use the remaining rue sprig to sprinkle the liquid (dip and flick) and repeat the chant. At the school gates is a good place, since the clique will pass through. Or try by their lockers or other regular haunts.

A word of warning about rue. It is quite common to have an allergic skin reaction when you come into contact with it, especially when it is wet. I always get a rash. So wear gloves if there is dew on plants or it has been raining, and keep your fingers out of the pot. Wear a glove when dipping and flicking.

If ingested in large quantities, rue can also make you ill. Don't allow anyone to drink any potion containing rue, ever. I'm trusting you. Break with the faith summed up in the *Wiccan Rede* – "An it harm none, do what ye will" – and the Threefold Law will strike. Whatever harm you cast out may return upon you, three times more powerful than your original intentions.

One last thing. Don't get caught casting this spell. It offers little protection from bold accusations of witchcraft. You could become the clique's next victim, if you're not already. Follow the witches' lore: "Be silent about your craft."

# Mutant bully stop poppet

Poppets – small dolls, effigies of individuals to act as a focus for a spell – have had a bad press. They're such visual aids that we've been treated to an endless supply of evil crones making models of their enemies and causing death with the help of a couple of sewing pins or hawthorns.

Wishing such harm is against the *Wiccan Rede*, whether you think pins and a poppet could do the trick or not.

Generally, witches use poppets for healing spells, and occasionally for binding somebody (stopping them from doing bad things), as is the case here. You must accept responsibility for all the possible outcomes of this spell, though, so treat and keep your poppet with care until the danger is passed – that is the bully's bullying days are over – and you can end the spell.

As well as making this poppet you should inform the relevant authorities about the bullying. Don't leave events to unfold naturally – somebody could get seriously hurt, or worse.

**cloth**
**as many of the following herbs as you**
**    can muster: rue, mugwort, vervain,**
**    lavender, rosemary, juniper berries**
**blue thread for stitching**
**white thread or ribbon for binding the**
**    poppet**

Some witches believe that including something of the bully, such as hair or nail clippings, helps when making an effigy (put it in with the stuffing), but others say embroidering the

person's name on the poppet is enough. You decide, bearing in mind that if this mutant bully is so scary, it might not be too easy to snaffle their DNA.

To make your poppet, cut out a front and back. On the front, embroider the person's name. Sew the two halves together leaving a small opening at the head so that you can stuff it. Once stuffed, stitch up the gap.

As you work speak this chant or make up a tune so that you can sing it: "I weave and mend with cloth and thread, to clear with spell the state of dread. I weave and mend, I mend and weave this spell so fear will take its leave."

When finished, take the white ribbon or thread and wind it around the poppet, saying, "With this thread I bind and halt the bully with a startled jolt. I wish no harm and no harm's done. But should they fight and try to harm the binding tightens on their arms. They shall not shout, they shall not stir, for with this thread I bind their power."

The poppet may now be placed in a box and stored in a freezer or dark cupboard until it is time to end the spell. You will know when the time is right. The bully will have apologized to everyone, explained that they have an unhappy homelife, that this is no excuse and go on to befriend their victims.

To end the spell, unbind the poppet, saying, "The time has come to let (person's name) go and so this spell it is undone." Unpick the stitches, pour out the herbs and cast into the wind, saying, "I thank the Spirit for this spell. I thank the Spirit for success. My heart is pure, my work is done, I go in peace with every breath."

# Things To bear in mind about bullying

• If people are cruel to animals they may well at some point be just as cruel to humans. Report all incidents of cruelty to animals to the relevant authorities.

• Bullies thrive on scaring people. If you show no fear, they won't pick on you.

• Allowing bullies to bully others is unacceptable. If you don't feel you can face up to a bully yourself – and you shouldn't if they are potentially dangerous – tell teachers or parents what is occurring.

·• If you are fearful that bullies are out to get you after school, get a parent or a friend's parent to give you a lift and tell them why (this is no time to worry about the environmental implications of car use on the school run).

• Never assume a bully will grow tired of bullying. Normally bullying tactics worsen.

• If you know of anybody carrying a dangerous weapon, report them (anonymously) immediately.

• Never assume that mental torture is any better than physical punch-ups. In many ways it's worse and in some cases can drive victims to suicide. Stand up to the mental bullies and if that fails, report them.

• All schools should have a bullying policy. Through your parents, ensure this policy is active and effective.

# Racism

You don't have to like everyone. But you can be polite. Deciding you don't like someone simply because your ancestors come from different parts of the world is ludicrous.

Living among a variety of cultures is fascinating and adds welcome variety.

There's nothing I like more at sabbats than welcoming folk from foreign climes. They always want to know what we're doing. Then they say, "Oh, we have a festival or saying for that." We ended up celebrating last Imbolg African-style with drums and chants. It was so energized, neighbours came out into their gardens and joined in. Magic!

As my dear mother always says, "Any one who is different from you probably has much to teach you. Speak little, listen much."

# Recreational drug use

It is understandable that as you break out from childhood, you will instinctively want to stick two fingers up at authority. Drugs represent a potently symbolic act and a readily available tool for such activity.

When you take drugs, your mind is altered. That's what drugs do. Under the influence you feel no emotional pain, your thoughts seem more profound than the Dalai Lama's and you have the courage to attempt many things that under normal circumstances you'd consider ill-advised or downright dangerous (unprotected sex, going home with strangers, getting into cars with drunk drivers, that sort of thing).

When the effects wear off, depending on our character we might accept that it was nothing but a dream, a nightmare or a mistake

and get on with life in the real world. Or we could take drugs again to perpetuate the illusion that "Hey, man, everything's cool."

But whether you're concerned about revision, or have a general malaise because "life is hopeless, and my parents don't understand me", drugs won't help you deal with the issues. They just make you forget about them until the comedown.

This is why drugs are so readily available to young people. To dealers, you and your peers represent an inexhaustible supply of eager new customers. You don't have the worldly experience fully to understand the downside of drugs and you are desperate to try new things – a curiosity driven by your hormones. Also, being a teenager is stressful at times. You will have problems you'd rather not think about.

To make it easier for the dealers, you tend to have routine lives. They know where to find you: school, play parks, nightclubs. Some dealers sell only cannabis. But there is a heck of a lot of money to be made from more addictive substances like speed, heroin and crack. The first time you're offered these it will be as a gift. "Try this," the friendly dealer will say. "On me. Let me know what you think. It's okay, I take it myself. Go on. What's the harm? It's only once. You're only trying it."

After a few "gifts" you will be expected to pay. That's when your troubles truly begin.

I'm not saying soft drugs, such as cannabis, automatically lead to hard drugs. This is simply untrue. But it is true that you might be exposed to harder drugs through dealers you meet through scoring cannabis. Unless you are clear in your mind – which can be difficult when you're stoned – you might find yourself in deeper waters than you planned. What

began as a quick dip into a subculture becomes a swim for your life through the dangerous currents of crime, squalor and degradation that always accompany a full-blown drug addiction.

When you can't resist the urge to rebel, try taking part in a non-violent environmental demonstration instead. It annoys the establishment just as much and it's better, long term, for your health and everyone else's.

Peer pressure introduces many to drugs. Peers don't always know what they're talking about though. So turn the page for the lowdown on commonly available drugs.

## Note to self

Because most recreational drugs are illegal, there is no official legislation governing quality or ingredients. Drugs may be contaminated with anything from rat poison to diesel fuel. There is no guarantee the product is organic, in fact I assume it's not – the plants that drugs are derived from could be sprayed with anything and generally are.

I may also be sold something totally different from what I requested, such as LSD or heroin instead of ecstasy. And I risk a criminal record if found to be carrying drugs.

As if this weren't problematical enough, drug production is controlled by drug and war lords. The growers receive a pittance. The big-money boys have fingers in all sorts of dodgy pies – arms deals, crooked governments, money laundering. When I buy drugs I support their causes.

## Tobacco

Due to 400,000 people dying every year from smoking-related illness, the tobacco industry is keen to attract new customers. Hey, how about it? You've seen the adverts – gorgeous people, stunning scenery, an exciting outdoor life. You want some of that, don't you?

Well, light up, then and not only will the scenery, your looks and your social life improve, but you'll be more grown-up, too. I have it on good authority – from the marketing manager of a cigarette company, actually. He says, "Smoking for the beginner is a symbolic act. I am no longer my mother's child, I'm tough, I am an adventurer, I'm not square."

However, he did add, "As the force from the psychological symbolism subsides, the pharmacological effect takes over to sustain the habit." Meaning: you're hooked, baby... ha ha ha ha. Cigarettes are more addictive than heroin. A smoking habit is harder to kick than a smack habit.

What that marketing manager failed to mention altogether was this:

• Growing tobacco is labour-intensive and takes up so much space that many farmers have no time and no spare land to grow food. They have to live on relief handouts from charities.

• Because tobacco growing is so labour-intensive, children are forced to work alongside their parents instead of going to school, even when schooling is free in their country.

• Forests are uprooted to supply fuel for curing tobacco leaves and building the curing houses. This means locals must walk further every day to collect firewood for cooking and in some areas the habitat of endangered species is destroyed to support the tobacco industry.

• Poor farmers often have to buy seed, pesticides and fertilizers from the same companies they sell the tobacco leaves to. It has been estimated that the average farmer in Brazil's Rio Azul region ends up owing the companies $500. Meanwhile the companies make $2 million just by selling the chemicals to the farmers in the first place.

• In Santa Catarina, Brazil, 79 per cent of tobacco growers have been poisoned by pesticides.

• Exposure to pesticides in Brazil has been linked to a dramatic rise in suicides among tobacco-farm workers. In the major tobacco-growing area of Rio Grande do Sul, suicide rates are nearly seven times the national average.

• Fertilizers and insecticides run off the fields and into nearby rivers, poisoning animals and people downstream.

• Tobacco plants suck up all the nutrients from soil. Once tobacco has been grown, few crops can thrive without the heavy use of fertilizers. This is often too expensive and land is left barren.

• Tobacco plants use so much water that they affect the local water tables, drying up wells in areas where it is grown. In hard times there is nothing to fall back on, since food stores and water supplies are diminished. Malawi in southern Africa, where at the time of writing there is famine, is a major tobacco-growing region.

If you can't avoid smoking for your own health, do it for God, Goddess and all the people, creatures and Elements who suffer through the addictive perpetuation of this senseless industry.

AMPHETAMINES

A white or pink powder also known as whizz, speed or poor man's cocaine (because it's cheaper). Speed increases the heart rate and breathing, creating general excitedness and a sense that everything has speeded up. Hence the name.

It is a drug favoured by the bored. Its use is rife among those excluded from school, and the unemployed living in badly designed "communities" lacking useful amenities.

The problems

Frequent use leads to poor skin, hair loss and low resistance to infections. Heavy users are spotty and bald with a constant cold, suffer unpredictable – often violent – mood swings and severe paranoia. The comedown is sharp, involving depression and lethargy. A voice inside the user's head says, "Take more drugs." This craving soon leads to addiction.

Healthy alternatives

Plan for a career in the health, fire or police services. Or train to be a teacher. Never a dull moment there. You'll be rushed off your feet and face genuine dramas on a daily basis.

CANNABIS

Derived from the female *Cannabis sativa* plant, this is the drug of choice for your parents' and grandparents' generation. Some of them probably still "skin up" to this day. Cannabis tends to make you giggle and have wild thoughts about life, the world and the universe. Unfortunately, post-comedown the precise details of your blinding moment of enlightenment are lost.

The problems

The…er….the…er…what are we talking about? Oh yes. Cannabis plays havoc with your short-term memory. So it's a useless pastime when you're supposed to be revising. Getting the munchies – a craving for snack foods, especially chocolate – is an occupational hazard and it's not called dope for nothing.

No one has ever died specifically of a cannabis overdose. But the drug is carcinogenic – meaning it can cause cancer. Since it is often mixed with tobacco in spliffs or joints, a little bit of experimenting could lead to a life-long nicotine habit with all the associated health implications.

Healthy
alternatives

Gardening brings about a similar state of mind. You live in the moment and dig, at one with nature and the world. A good film, book or play will also take you out of yourself and into the realms of waking dreams.

CRACK

When my mother travelled through Peru she suffered from altitude sickness. This occurs in mountainous regions where the air is thinner, containing less oxygen than lower-lying areas.

Her guide recommended coca leaves, which she drank as a tea. The indigenous peoples of South America have long realized the healing properties of coca. So socially acceptable is coca-leaf tea that it was served in urns at her hotels. "It definitely helped," says Mother. "It pepped me up. But the effect didn't last long. I had to drink three cups in one sitting and I kept needing more." My mother!

Crack cocaine is a white powder derived from coca leaves. First coke is made using a variety of substances including petrol and ether (no, it's not eco-friendly or body-friendly). This powder is cooked with baking powder to form white lumps which are smoked, giving a bigger, more instant hit than cocaine. This hit wears off quickly.

The problems

Where to start? Following an intense, allegedly pleasurable high, lasting around half an hour with appetite and tiredness suppressed, there's one almighty comedown. The user feels tired, anxious, depressed, with a headache and pains all over the body. The only way to stave off the comedown, or crash as it's called, is to take more crack.

To fund habits, users mug old ladies, burgle homes and steal people's trainers and mobile phones. Because crack makes users aggressive, violent and manic, they think nothing of coshing their victims over the head. Female users often fund their habit through prostitution, a desperate business.

Crack has become increasingly associated with heroin use. The heroin helps with the initial crash, but long term only adds to the problems.

Healthy
alternatives

Take a course in parachute jumping if you enjoy high-octane risks. Horse-riding and mountaineering are also suitably dangerous and thrilling. But do receive proper training before setting out to conquer Everest or win an Olympic show-jumping medal.

**ECSTASY OR MDMA**

MDMA was once prescribed to married couples experiencing relationship difficulties. It helped them to relate. It wasn't long before its recreational uses were realized and it was promptly banned.

Did that stop its use? Did it heck. Now known as E, holiday destinations have developed to cater for users and clubs have become churches for the drug's worshippers. In the UK the E culture appears to be the main sales outlet for the bottled water industry.

Ecstasy causes users to enjoy rhythmic repetitive movement. It plays games with our sensory perceptions, which means our experience of light and sound is changed.

**The problems**

Because E raises the body temperature, and users like to dance non-stop for hours, overheating is a common danger. So it is recommended that users sip a pint of water over every hour while high and take time out in chill zones to cool down and lower the heart rate.

Drinking too much water, however, has proven fatal in rare cases, as has an allergy to the drug itself. Although allergy to aspirin is more common, every life lost is a tragedy.

Non-fatal side-effects include sweating, nausea and vomiting, increased heart rate, dizziness and jaw tension which leads to jaw grinding and worn-down teeth.

Little is known about the long-term effects on health because the drug hasn't been around long enough. But preliminary research suggests that ecstasy causes liver, kidney, heart and possibly brain damage, depression, anxiety and other mental health problems.

If a friend is taken ill, call an ambulance and seek immediate help from responsible adults. Any drugs left over after the collapse should be handed over to medical staff, since lives can more easily be saved if doctors know what they're dealing with.

**Healthy alternatives**

Learn to dance the tarantella. It's a very fast dance, involving leaps, fancy footwork and banging a tambourine. Traditionally it is repetitive and long – the dancer dances until they drop. It was believed that if you had been bitten by a tarantula spider, by dancing the tarantella you'd work the poison out of your system.

HEROIN

Heroin nullifies all pain and creates a euphoric sense of well-being. That's why morphine, which like heroin is derived from the opium poppy, is used to treat cancer patients. It doesn't cure, but it does make the terminally ill comfortable.

The problems

As a recreational drug it's hopeless because it's highly addictive. Once taken, the brain demands ever-increasing amounts of heroin just so you can feel "normal". This requires a constant supply.

To support a habit users steal, prostitute themselves and deal – spreading the misery to others. Rich kids might not have financial constraints, but it is possible to die of an overdose or contract HIV or hepatitis C (both potentially fatal conditions) if needles are shared. Coming off heroin without medical help can lead to wild, frightening hallucinations, pain all over the body and the worst diarrhoea you could imagine. Worse even. Many users go back to their habit just to ease these symptoms.

Heroin smokers may spare themselves the risk of AIDS and liver cancer (caused by hepatitis C), but they still end up with their teeth dropping out and smelling of urine.

Healthy alternatives

Choose life.

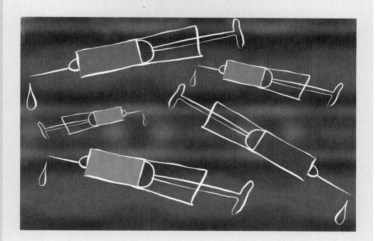

**LSD OR ACID**

Big news in the late 1960s, it was as influential on popular culture as E was in the 1990s. The drug is powerfully hallucinogenic. The psychedelic dream experience it causes is called a trip. When it's a nightmare rather than a dream, it's called a bad trip.

**The problems**

It isn't addictive but it's heavy going on the old brain cells. Anyone with mental health problems should steer clear. Actually you might not realize you have a problem until you drop (swallow) the tab. That's when any lurking psychotic or schizophrenic tendencies make themselves known. And it won't end when you come down. That's it. You might find yourself locked up in a mental institution.

Another problem is that the effects of the drug vary depending on who you're with, where you are and how you were feeling prior to taking acid. On a good trip you might think you can talk to the animals, taste smells and hear colours. On a bad trip you might think giant spiders are crawling up your body intent on eating your head. You might also believe you can fly. This is fine if you attempt take off from the ground but not if you leap from a bridge or tall building as is the way with some LSD victims.

Whichever way the trip goes, once you're on it you can't get off for up to 24 hours. If you've ever been to festivals and seen people acting in a totally bonkers fashion, screaming at monsters only they can see – that's acid.

**Healthy alternatives**

Read Tom Wolfe's novel *The Electric Cool Aid Acid Test.*

# Alcohol

Imbibing alcohol is an ancient tradition among humans. It was once believed that the feelings it created were of a spiritual rather than a physical nature. Alcohol was drunk at temples (and still is) as part of the ritual of worship.

Alcohol now plays a major role in many celebrations, be it a family gathering, a party or a festival. It's what humans do.

(No)alternatives like their drinks to be natural. The three favourites are organic cider, organic ale and organic wine. Witches don't drink prior to casting spells since it affects concentration and therefore weakens the mental and magical powers.

## The problems

The acceptance of social drinking has led to widespread "over-drinking" – that is, drinking more than is good for the liver and the soul. Drinking after work, or when the kids are in bed, has become a necessity for many people, who find it helps them to unwind from the rigours of the day. Having a hangover the following morning simply adds stress to their lives, which must be counteracted by more drink the following evening. This is how a drinking habit develops.

Young people are encouraged down this path by the promise that alcohol will make them braver, happier, sexier, more successful – or whatever virtue the advertisers think will appeal to you the consumer at the time.

Drinking frees you up, makes you feel brave, gives you the impression that you could rule the world – unless your team loses, in which case it triggers anger and depression.

While drinking itself is tolerated, the behaviour it induces, especially among the young, is becoming increasingly unacceptable to many. Because it releases us from our inhibitions, otherwise perfectly reasonable individuals find themselves fighting, stealing cars and/or driving while drunk, having sex without using condoms, trying drugs they hadn't planned to and vomiting in the back of their best friend's dad's car (when he has a long business trip to make the following day – yeauch). They may also try to kiss their best friend's dad and wake up the following day with absolutely no inkling of what's gone on. Until they're reminded.

The best advice I can give you is to drink only organic wines, ales and ciders which are natural products and don't seem to induce violence or vomiting in the same way that lager and alcopops do.

The reason alcopops make you vomit is that different brands contain different types of alcohol. You start with one made from tequila, follow it up with a vodka-based drink and round that off with a non-descript alcohol which defies definition on the bottle. Mix your drinks and your stomach will complain spectacularly.

Here follow a few helpful tips of those of you who drink – with or without your parents' permission.

• Don't feel you have to drink alcohol just because everyone else seems to be doing it.

• Alternate alcoholic drinks with the same amount of non-alcoholic liquid, preferably water. It will help your liver and head enormously.

• Never mix the grape (wine) and the grain (beer or spirits).

• Avoid fruit punch at parties. It's often laced with spirits and more than one person might think it's funny to add more spirits. This makes for a potent drink, as you will realize when the room – or is it you – begins to wobble.

• When drinking outdoors or indoors, always dispose of containers thoughtfully. Leaving glass bottles or cans lying around can injure humans and animals. The plastic loops which hold cans together can choke small mammals and birds.

• Recycle all bottles and cans and avoid plastic altogether if you can.

• If you give yourself a hangover, drink peppermint tea and plenty of water. Eating grapefruit seems to help. You can also buy grapefruit essential oil. Heat five drops on a burner, inhale and apologize to your head and liver.

• If you feel sick in a car, ask the driver to stop so you can get out. Alternatively wind down the window and lean out (when the car has stopped). Don't vomit in cars. You lose a lot of friends that way.

# A perfect party plan

Parties are wonderful things. At least they can be, so long as you plan carefully, stick to your plan and have a contingency plan ready for when the plan goes wrong.

Yep, a good party is all in the planning. But first, you have to get permission from your parents. This is always easier if they consider you to be responsible, mature and likely to clear up afterwards.

If this isn't how your parents see you, perhaps you could persuade them to give you the chance to prove yourself. Then prove it.

Down to the plans. First you need…

### …the excuse

Birthdays and religious festivals, especially pagan sabbats, are perfect excuses for perfect parties. Pagans love to party. It gives us the chance to acknowledge the turning of the wheel of the year, welcoming the change of seasons and the gifts that each brings. It's also a chance to gather with friends and the occasional stranger, which creates a magical power as human spirits join together in celebration.

On page 222 you'll find all the dates and excuses you'll ever need for a party.

## Budget

Working within a budget is an essential life skill. You don't need a bottomless pit of cash to throw a good party. A little can go a long way if you're smart. Friends are usually only too happy to contribute by bringing a plate of food each. Do guide them though, otherwise you might end up with 37 bags of crisps, five plates of sausages on sticks, three lumps of cheese and no bread.

Alcohol can suck a budget dry. If people want it suggest they bring their own. Or decide on a no-alcohol policy – excessive drinking by even one guest can send the entire party off onto a totally unwanted orbit.

Put a little bit of money aside for practical party equipment (see list below) and then work out how many guests your budget can cover. The venue will help you determine this.

## Top Tip

Whatever you do, do not attempt to throw a party at home without informing your parents. Your karmic account will be running on overdraft. Everything, I mean *everything* that could go wrong will go wrong, plus all the things that couldn't possibly go wrong will go wrong as well. To cut a long story short your parents will never forgive you and will never trust you again… ever…about anything. Nothing. Oh, and you'll be grounded.

# Venue

In the summer, gardens, parks, beaches and woodland are all excellent choices. But what if it rains? Make sure your plans can be suitably translated. Thirty guests in the garden is relaxing. Thirty guests in your bedroom (because your parents value their living-room carpet) is a game of sardines. Which might not be the end of the world and you'll certainly all know each other better by the end of the evening.

So be realistic, but dream a little. You may just get the perfect hazy summer day for your birthday barbecue of midsummer revelry.

Choose a date when you know your friends will be available. Friday or Saturday nights are best, unless it's holiday time, since you and your chums are more likely to be allowed a late night. Avoid dates when half your class are away on a school trip or when a popular band has a gig in your area.

Fancy dress can enliven a party because costumes break the ice. Themed fancy dress provides an added challenge. It means they can't just go out and hire their usual gorilla costume. "Who I was in a past life" works well (prepare for several Cleopatras and a smattering of Napoleons). Other good themes include Moons and Stars, Gods and Goddesses, Witches and Wizards or Romans and Druids. I often invite my guests to wear certain colours – orange and black for Halloween, green for boys and white for girls for Beltane.

# Deck The halls

Make your own bunting. It's really easy. Cut triangles out of old wrapping paper or anything to hand, join them together with string and hang.

Stars and moon mobiles are cool, too. Paint onto cardboard and hang on threads from the ceiling (high enough not to annoy guests, or tempt them to pull). Most of the sabbats have traditions and decor associated with each festival such as carved pumpkins for Halloween and decorated trees and greenery for Yule. Hindus' Diwali is fun with candles and chalk drawings on the floor (it comes off easily, but is probably not a good idea on carpets).

Candles – beeswax of course – are always lovely, but need to be watched carefully. Tealights in jam jars are the safest, but make sure there's a heat-proof dish or a drink mat between the jar and the surface it's placed on. If you can't find or afford beeswax, be wary of lighting too many household candles. One Imbolg I lit my home with cheap white candles. It looked stunning, but two guests had asthma attacks.

Commercially grown cut flowers can be beautiful, but tend to be expensive and environmentally unsound. They're grown in huge greenhouses, using lots of energy, fertilizer and pesticide, which cause health problems for growers and florists. The flowers are often flown halfway around the world. Planes are a major contributor to greenhouse gases, climate change and the hole in the ozone layer. It's best if your flowers come attached to a plant, grown in your country or, better still, straight from your garden.

You may wish to heat oils or incense for added ambience. Don't overdo it with the incense, though, as some guests may find the smoke unpleasant. Certain essential oils should be avoided altogether. Rosemary in particular could cause unpleasant side effects for anyone with high blood pressure. Eucalyptus, geranium and lemon are no good for anyone with diabetes. If you have an epileptic friend, avoid basil, eucalyptus, fennel or rosemary. Lavender could be good, or bergamot. But I have come across people who are allergic to lavender. Poor things.

## Essential life tool number 5 Music

Music allows us to express emotions and ideas that otherwise might go unexpressed. A life without music, especially live music, would be like life without air, food, water or love. A party without music isn't a party.

We all have our favourite bands and singers. If you like popular chart music you and your friends will enjoy dancing around and singing along together. This can be very powerful. It's like at live gigs when the whole crowd moves as one. I was at a U2 concert once and the sense of connection between the crowd and the band will stay with me forever. It was magic.

At parties I prefer to play old records rather than CDs. The crackling and the age of the songs create a welcoming, comforting sort of ambience. Second-hand record players and records are just so cheap to come by these days. Recycled music. Great! The price of needles is steep, though, because there's not much demand for them.

If you haven't got records, I'm sure you have access to CDs. World music is different if you're not a chart fan. Anything from African drumming to gypsy violins, via Latin American

salsa is guaranteed to get the party in a dancing mood. Dancing is excellent. It transcends all cultural and language barriers. Like singing and drumming it's a universal activity. It allows us all to understand that we share Spirit. If we can dance together we can do anything together.

Drumming is the heartbeat. Songs originated in the sounds of nature. We mimicked them. We ordered the sounds. We learned to communicate with the world and between each other. These are some of the reasons witches and (no)alternatives like dancing, singing and drumming.

Acoustic music is best. You won't need an electricity supply, amp or speakers. Which means you can enjoy it any time and anywhere, from a hill top to the garden, a park or the beach.

Drums, dulcimers, fiddles, harmonicas, penny whistles, guitars and banjos are all possibles, so long as the musicians can play. If you're at all musical, get learning an instrument or collecting songs. It's what witches do. If you are about as musical as a brick make friends with musicians. They represent a unique brand of humanity to be welcomed to your heart and hearth.

If you're lacking real instruments and expert musicians, try this: get a pile of logs, all different widths and lengths. Each will have a different tone which makes for some interesting rhythm sequences. You can also use dustbin lids, a watering can with a length of hose attached or a tea-chest, broom and string, to make a home-made bass. Bottles and jars with different amounts of water in them can be fun. You are limited musically only by your imagination.

# Note to self

I will not play loud music with a thumping bass at my parties. While I and friends might be enjoying it, my neighbours and their neighbours can only hear the thump thump thump which is most unsettling, since it tends to be electronic and have no soul. Real drums are not half so annoying. Those who run scared of real drumming are running scared from their true selves, from nature, from the red thread that links all through time and space. Unless it's after midnight, in which case they might just be wanting to sleep, which is fair enough if you have to get up for work early the following day.

# Cake and ale

Some witches use the phrase cake and ale in reference to grounding food used after power has been raised in spell work and ritual. It stops people coming over all nauseous and dizzy.

At the drop-in coven we use cake and ale as slang for sabbat catering. It can be simple but should vary from what we eat on a daily basis since it is, after all, a celebration. It is practical to keep to vegetarian dishes served as finger foods, such as dips with fresh chopped vegetables and bite-sized munchies. Guacamole, humous, pizza and salsa are perfect and recipes are easy to come by. The host or hostess and helpful friends can then mingle with the guests proffering plates heaped with goodies.

This style of cake and ale saves you the effort of dealing with sink-loads of washing up. You won't have all those individual plates

and cutlery to cope with. Paper and plastic plates and cups are a big green no-no, a terrible waste of natural resources,

Trays covered with vine leaves or tea towels make great platters. A friend recommends banana leaves as an unusual alternative – but I don't have a banana tree in my garden. You might, though.

# The parent problem

Should they stay or should they go? If you're new to hosting parties, keep them hanging around in the background. They have their uses. They will point out that the burning smell is the charred remains of your pizzas and help keep the noise within acceptable limits – although since grown-ups tend to err on the side of caution, you may not thank them for their views on volume control.

If you keep your parents at home, your friends' parents will be happier to let your mates party on for longer.

Party-throwing veterans might be able to persuade parents to vacate the building. But have a contact number for them just in case the house gets overrun with drunken gatecrashers, who can do a lot of damage to your reputation, not to mention your parents' furniture, in a very short space of time.

# Good host and hostess practice

Your job is to ensure that everyone has a good time – that's what parties are for. Make sure no one's good time is at the expense of others, whether it be other guests, your neighbours, family pets or those involved in the post-party mopping up operation. Therefore:

✳ Always inform neighbours when you're throwing a party. That way they can choose to go out to avoid the inevitable noise. A good way to placate neighbours is to invite them round for pre-party drinks. If your parents get on with them, maybe they'll leave with them. Having your parents just next door is possibly the perfect place for them to be.

✳ For the first hour or so, at least, be available to greet guests as they arrive.

✳ Organize a suitable place for guests to drop off their coats.

✳ Ensure that everyone is offered a drink and something to eat soon after they arrive.

✳ Don't leave people standing around on their own. Introduce wallflowers to your chattiest friends, but be prepared to rescue them if they appear overwhelmed.

✳ Don't play music too loudly – people begin to shout to be heard. The dancers then turn the music up to hear it over the shouters. The shouters have to shout louder and soon the cacophony is unbearable.

✳ Have a quiet room as well as a dancing room if you can.

✳ If your parents' bedroom is out of bounds, put a sign on the door stating this fact. If the door can't be locked, check it out occasionally. Be firm should you find your parents' bed occupied. Your parents have trusted you. Don't blow it.

✳ Use signs to indicate where the toilets are.

✳ Ensure that family pets have a safe sanctuary away from the noise and bustle.

✳ Clear up as you go along and you'll have an easier task at the end of the evening. Plus your guests will enjoy a tidy environment more than one caked in party debris.

✳ Only use candles if they can be placed in safe positions, well away from curtains and elbows.

✳ Have the following close to hand:

**separate containers (labelled) for glass, cans, plastic, paper and compost to make recycling easier the following day**
t**he telephone number of a taxi firm (a sign placed by the telephone, accompanied by the address of the party, is helpful)**
**plenty of toilet rolls**
**a bucket, cloth and disinfectant (work it out)**
**suitable eco-friendly cleaning materials for drink and food spills on the carpets and upholstery**
**washing-up liquid and clean tea towels**
**napkins (cloth ones may be bought cheaply at charity shops) and finger bowls for guests**

## Perfect party spell

If you've followed my instructions and you, your guests and your parents vaguely behave themselves, you should have a perfect party. Just to help things a long a little, try this spell.

**2 bowls**
**flower petals**
**floating candles**

Place a bowl with petals and candles on either side of your front door. Stand looking in towards the house and say, "May our meeting be merry, our moot be gay, may this party be blessed in every way. I call on the spirit to grant us all, love, peace and friendship. Let that be our call. And when it is time to wend our ways home, may the Spirit protect us where'er we must roam." Draw a pentacle on your door. The spell is cast. Let the revelries begin.

## Spell Tip

Candles won't stay alight unless they're sheltered from winds. Using high-sided bowls with less water offers some protection.

# Travel

You probably don't have much say in where your family goes on holiday. But before your parents do put a cross by the holiday destination of their choice, could you point out that each person on a long-haul return flight is responsible for the same amount of $CO_2$ emissions as the average motorist in the UK causes over a year.

And despite recent improvements in the state of the ozone layer, scientists predict that by 2015 half of its annual destruction will be caused by air travel.

I could go on, but I won't. Instead, let me introduce you to the writings of Shiram Jaiswal. This true story is printed with his kind permission. It is from a home-published anthology of his work, titled *In Quest of a Remedy and Other Stories*. Details of how to get hold of a copy can be found on page 232.

He learned to write in English, having had only three and a half years of formal schooling, by asking travellers to correct his work. The story might seem predictable. This is because it's so familiar. So familiar that many of us fail even to notice this sort of thing any more.

Over to Shiram:

The real voyage of discovery consists not in seeking new landscapes but in having new eyes.

Marcel Proust

## Lake of Joy

(*This is the lake at Mirik, a three-hour bus ride from Darjeeling.*)

Once, far from the maddening crowd of the city, there was a lake in a fragrant alpine forest in the Himalayas. In this natural environment various kinds of birds and beasts lived in verdant surroundings, full of flower and song. The crystal-clear waters of the placid lake sparkled in the sunlight. These waters brought heavenly charms to the earth when the azure sky and the scenic beauty of the mountains were reflected on the surface of the lake.

Tired of the hustle and bustle of the city, trekkers would come here to unwind and enjoy sylvan charms. The very sight of the lake and the surrounding lush green landscape would invigorate them and relieve them of their fatigue. They would gaze spellbound upon the majestic trees and listen with rapture to the sweet songs of birds, feeling at one with nature. When these nature lovers eventually went home they told everyone they met about this beautiful lake, the "Lake of Joy".

Drawn by the peace and bounty of the lake, more and more people began to visit this place of unspoiled natural harmony. The government found that the place had immense potential for tourism and so plans were initiated to develop it.

This development programme required rapid deforestation. A rich forest of thousands of *Cryptomeria japonica* trees was cleared in order to make way for buildings which would provide accommodation for those nature lovers seeking discoveries beyond their daily lives. Concrete housing for construction workers was erected beside the lake, depriving birds and beasts of their habitats. In this once-relaxing atmosphere, trinket and souvenir

shops, restaurants and tea stalls began to appear. Taxis and buses started to reach the lake. Honking and shouting replaced the birdsong and the clamour of crowds now overwhelmed the rhythmic sounds of nature.

In order to further develop the placid and pleasant environment of the lake into a "real attraction", a low concrete wall painted green and topped with barbed wire was constructed to encircle the water. Using explosives to remove the rocks, a wide path was built around the lake along the wall, and the hill was reinforced with concrete at great cost.

Flower baskets were hung at regular intervals along the paths to give the tourists a pleasant natural environment as they walked. However, all these baskets found their way into the homes of the local people before it was possible to see the first blooms of spring.

Hundreds of people were employed to manage what became a "beautiful" tourist spot. In order to maintain the natural beauty which had previously existed for thousands of years with no help from anyone, the Forest Department hacked out clearings in the wilderness to facilitate the building of its offices.

In spite of financial constraints, 50 people were given the job of scraping the moss away from the retaining walls under the supervision of yet another five workers. Beautification, however, did not serve to strengthen the structures. With the start of the monsoon rains, much of the construction began to deteriorate due to the low quality of the materials used. Later, mounds of rubbish gathered at every corner of this "tourist attraction" as the number of street sweepers proved insufficient.

The government had failed to make suitable arrangements for cleaning this tourist "paradise" owing to insufficient funds, yet it allocated money to provide more attractions to promote tourism. These included a zoo with small cages and a park – the highest Amusement Park in the world – to provide suspense and thrills never experienced before.

A little way up the other hill, they cut down rhododendrons, camellias, dahlias and other wildflower trees and here they planted different flowers – flowers which could be seen at their visitors' homes. This was done so that visitors' families could feel at home and could gather to enjoy a placid, peaceful moment of life, taking delight in western music blaring through the loudspeakers, which were put up by the Department of Tourism in order to create a healthy and eco-friendly tourist destination.

On the great occasion of its inauguration, a grand meeting was arranged at which a speech on "environmental awareness" was to be delivered. In order to facilitate the traffic, the road was extended on either side by the cutting down of more trees. Now the environmentalists could arrive easily in their cars provided by the government and Worldwide Fund for Nature.

Further down on the bank of the lake lay an overturned skip spilling its rubbish straight into the lake that once brought a smile to the eyes of visitors. Nearby open drains poured out foul-smelling pollutants turning the waters so black that the sun ceased to dance upon them. The smiling face of the lake which brought joy to all creatures had faded and its allure gone.

The "Lake of Joy", a piece of paradise on earth, was lost – all in the name of "beautification". Its water, once so pure and clear, which quenched the thirst of the mind, had become putrid and stagnant. The filth on its surface shrouded the pristine glory and tranquillity of the lake. An old rusty signpost, standing like a tombstone by its shore, read:

"Protect the lake for the joy of others."

# Camping

Witches and (no)alternatives can't abide hotels. We prefer to carry a rucksack on our backs with a tent and sleeping bag attached. We can follow our heart or the map and either way we're guaranteed an adventure. And so long as we take our rubbish away with us, our eco-footprint is minimal. It's so much more exciting than hotels.

When I was a young girl we lived in a tent for a while. Without the barrier of bricks and mortar my spirit was able to soar. The family got a taste for this and we would choose to spend our summers in this way, even when we did have the use of a perfectly good roof over our heads.

Days would be spent gathering wild foods like herbs (my mother's an expert – don't try eating anything you don't totally recognize, you might get poisoned), seaweeds and shellfish (the seas were marginally cleaner and healthier back in the 1970s, or so we thought). We cooked, we ate, we washed, we talked, we sang and we played al fresco, rising with the dawn and snuggling into our sleeping bags as the sun set, which is quite late in summer.

This allowed us to tune into the natural rhythms of the day and night. It gave me a great complexion and I met some truly fascinating people. I also got to star-gaze, worship the moon in all her phases and feel the dew beneath my feet – three activities guaranteed to improve spell casting, give you an unquenchable appetite for life and the ability to use initiative in face of adversity. Camping is character building.

We still hark back to these freedom days at the drop-in coven. On warm nights, preferably before an esbat (a celebration of the full moon), we camp out by the herb garden. We would never dream of touring any other way.

If you're at all disenchanted with modern living, get out "there" in a tent. It's the perfect antidote to the fast, electronically driven way of life that has come to be seen as "normal".

## Essential life Tools number 6 Camping gear

To be a truly happy camper you will need the following:

**tent**
**sleeping bag**
**sensible clothing**
**sun block**
**water bottle**
**minimal medical kit**
**camping cakes and ale.**
**solar/wind-up powered torch and radio**
**rucksack**

## Tent

Most parents will allow you to camp in the garden – or a mate's garden – even if they won't let you set off alone across a continent. If you ever plan to attend a music and arts or environmental festival, such as the Big Green Gathering, going without a tent would be like going without toilet paper. Tents are also very useful on picnics, giving shade and shelter from changes in the weather and the wind.

Purists often prefer benders (made from bent birch branches and covered with tarpaulin), yurts (round canvas and wood constructions) or tipis (straight poles and canvas, as used by Native American Indians) to

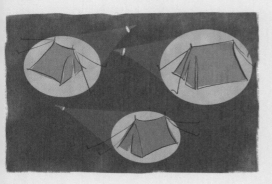

modern tents. It's a growing market. Ask around and, if it's the right moment, you will meet people who can help you.

• The latest models are light-weight and easy to erect. If buying second-hand, get the person selling it to put it up. That way you'll know all the poles and pegs are present, the zips work and there aren't any holes – climb inside and have a look. If daylight's getting through, so will rain.

• Never put tents away damp – they go mouldy. If you have to pack it up in the rain, dry it out thoroughly when you get home.

• If you are intent on lighting a fire, keep it as far away from tents as possible (the sparks may not set it alight, although they can, but they may well burn holes). Never use naked flames in a tent for obvious reasons.

• Keep tents zipped up before twilight to prevent dew descending on sleeping bags. Keeping them closed will also keep bugs and critters at bay.

• Keep guy ropes as short as possible so that there's less danger of tripping over them in the dark. That "twang" followed quickly by a thud and a groan – I only have to imagine it and I laugh, but it's not funny at the time.

• If you know there is a potential problem with poisonous snakes or insects, seek advice from a local wildlife warden on minimizing risks.

## Sleeping bag

Go for the best tog rating you can afford. The higher it is, the warmer the bag will be. Sleeping bags aren't just for camping expeditions. They're perfect for sleep-overs and easier to transport than a duvet or quilt.

When camping, you'll also need a ground mat for comfort and warmth – one layer beneath you is worth three on top.

## Suitable clothing

However warm the day, once the sun goes down it can get cold, especially when there are no insulating clouds to hold in warmth.

Your clothing, therefore, should be layers of natural materials which can be added on or removed according to temperature. Cotton, hemp, silk and wool are the best, with waxed clothing for rainy days. But there are plenty of synthetic waterproof materials around if you can't afford a waxed poacher's coat (lots of pockets big enough to carry a pheasant, or notebooks) and waxed trousers.

You should also have a couple of hats at your disposal. One to keep your head warm and one to shade your face.

Shoes should be leather, sturdy, suitable for walking and keep your feet warm and dry.

# Note To self

In warm dry weather barefoot is the most natural way to walk, but isn't always safe, owing to glass and other nasties being left lying around by thoughtless others. If it's too hot for sturdy shoes I can wear a lighter summer version, such as Birkenstock. Fashion styles, don't offer much protection and are inherently sexist. They prevent girls being able to enjoy all sorts of activities that boys take for granted. They also cause corns, blisters and back problems because our bodies are not "designed" to cater for high heels.

# Medical kit

A few plasters or clean cotton hankies (wrapped and knotted) keep cuts and grazes free from dirt.

A bottle of lavender oil – useful for disinfecting wounds and can be applied neat to the skin.

Sunblock – the ozone layer isn't what it once was – a protective layer in the stratosphere that stops us getting frazzled by the sun's rays. Thanks to the ban on CFC

sprays and the ongoing battle to dismantle old fridges with care, things have improved somewhat, but are still far from perfect. So slap on the cream, paying particular attention to your nose, shoulders, ears and any bits that don't get exposed too often.

Midge and mosquito repellents – burn citronella candles or heat the oil – but not in the tent itself. Eucalyptus oil (8 drops) mixed with 16 ml/3 teaspoons vodka can be shaken well then applied to the skin. If you can't buy vodka and an adult doesn't trust you on your intended use, try almond oil instead.

If you do get bites, mix baking powder with water to make a paste and rub on.

# Camping cakes and ale

For all possible camping catering needs you will need only the following:

**a small gas ring, storm kettle or fire**
**a small saucepan**
**a metal cup**
**a knife (for buttering bread and cutting cheese)**
**a water bottle**
**a bowl and spoon**

On short trips you can survive on bread, cheese, fruit, raw vegetables and nuts. But if you want warming foods, try porridge (adding fruit) or baked beans with a boiled egg. A small gas ring is easy if you have access to gas cylinders. Alternatively, use a storm kettle, which relies on wood and kindling.

A good metal water bottle will last for years, if not a lifetime, and means you'll never go short of a refreshing glug of water, whether you're venturing into the outback or simply going to school.

## Lumos

Mine and three other people's lives were once saved by my tiny torch. We were caught out camping on a dry river bed (Doh!). It was raining in the mountains upstream. Whoosh came the water. We used the torch to help us pick our way across rocks and to safety. Phew!

A torch will also help to scare away wild beasties if they're of the human-eating variety. Light is magical – think how much we rely on it – which is probably why the Lumos spell featured so heavily in J. K. Rowling's Harry Potter books.

You can now buy excellent wind-up torches, which are just as magical as waving a wand.

Some have solar panels and double up as a radio. There's a contact address in the back of the book (see Freeplay, page 235), but camping shops might also be able to help. Batteries are polluters and not energy-efficient.

## Rucksack

Even on long trips everything you are likely to need can be packed into one rucksack. They often have lots of side pockets for storing items like passports, money, snacks or water (if you take the rucksack off, keep valuables on your person) and straps for holding your sleeping bag.

If you can't fit everything in, take a third out. Really, you won't use it.

## Note To self

If I get caught short I will have to take advantage of Nature's strategically placed bushes. If I need anything more serious than a pee, I will dig a hole and bury it.

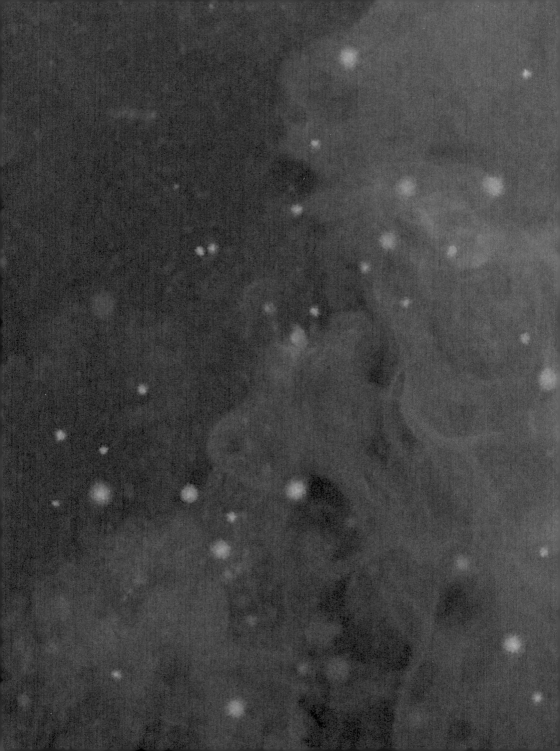

When we embark upon the journey to redefine our relationship with our world, we inevitably meet with dissent. We are told our contribution is so tiny it is of no importance. We are told it's too late to save the world, so why bother? We are told there might be time to save the world but unless everybody joins in, it won't work.

How do we respond? We hold out our hands and wait for others to grasp them. We hope that eventually every hand of every human will join in love, friendship and a desire to be good ancestors. We lead by example. We do our bit and more. And we chant together, "*Yichallal, Yichallal, Yichallal.*" *Yichallal* is an Ethiopian word meaning "It is possible and it can be done."

Be hopeful, be loving, have courage and endurance. For then we will be rewarded by the greatest shift in human thinking and feeling in the history of our species' time on this planet.

We can be the solution. We can.

*Yichallal*, young witches. Let all our hearts travel together on our individual paths until our minds meet as one.

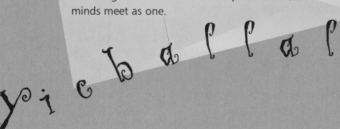

# Sabbats, festivals and other holy days

This is by no means a comprehensive list of all festivals. The following are just a few that speak to us from the past, despite a couple of them arising out of the tail end of the twentieth century. What they have in common is that they all have something to say about our future.

Celebrating the seasons and the position of the moon and the sun helps us to understand the natural rhythms that hold power over our way of life. It also provides plenty of perfect excuses for parties.

### Tu B'Shevat (fifteenth day of the Hebrew month of Shevat – sometime in January by the Gregorian calendar)

Jewish Earth Day. In Israel they plant trees. Further north it's too cold – saplings may be killed by frost if planted at this time. Light a candle in memory of all the trees that have been felled for profit with no thought to the genuine needs of the present or the future. Go hug one. Send a donation to the International Tree Foundation or Tree Spirit (details on pages 235 and 237).

### World Religion Day (sometime in January)

Organized by the Baha'i, an offshoot of Islam, this day is dedicated to the unity and oneness of all world religions. Celebrate with an interfaith service.

### Imbolg (2 February)

One of the four major pagan sabbats. Time to be planting seeds – the week of the full moon is best – it may be before or after Imbolg. Fill your home (safely) with candles. Admire the snowdrops. A great time for planning how your garden will look come summer. Life is stirring within the earth – spring's on her way.

### Easter and Ostara (March to April)

Both festivals, the former Christian the latter pagan, celebrate the arrival of spring, rebirth and resurrection. They share common symbols and activities such as decorated eggs, flower bonnets and the hare (now more likely to be described as an Easter bunny) which is an ancient Egyptian fertility icon. It is also a symbol of the moon.

Easter is held on the first Sunday after the full moon following the vernal equinox on 21 March. Ostara is always held on 21 March. Both festivals take their name from Eostre, the Anglo-Saxon Goddess of spring. Easter is the only lunar-based festival in the Christian calendar.

### Holi (sometime in March by the Gregorian calendar – it moves with the moon)

The Hindu harvest festival. In hot, dry countries where rain is more a seasonal thing than a weekly unpredictable thing, it is not surprising that water plays a major part in a harvest celebration. Hindus traditionally have water fights and smear each other with coloured powders. Enjoy, but clean up after yourselves.

## Earth Day (22 April)

Happy Earth Day to you. All around the world events are held on this day to celebrate our natural world and promote its care. You could organize an organic food festival or a tree-planting session or launch a neighbourhood recycling scheme. You could clear out a pond, create a wildlife garden or do a sponsored walk in aid of gorillas. You decide. The Earth Day network has plenty of ideas to inspire.

For (no)alternatives every day is Earth Day, but this important festival, which has been growing annually for the last three decades, means a lot to those working towards a cleaner, safer, happier world for all. Get involved.

## Yom Hashoah (sometime in April or early May)

Jewish Holocaust Day was established to remember the six million Jews killed by the Nazis in 1933-45. It is celebrated by Jews and non-Jews alike. Everyone who has ever been persecuted or murdered for their race, their beliefs or their physical differences may also be remembered and mourned. Light seven candles and heat cedarwood oil on a burner to encourage a more spiritual attitude to our fellow human beings. This should never be allowed to happen again. And yet it goes on.

## Beltane (30 April/1 May)

Some celebrate May Day eve, some the day itself. In these uncertain climatic times we allow the weather to decide, for it is best to be outdoors to welcome the summer in. Traditional activities include dancing round a maypole – or any type of dancing, in a park, in the streets or out in unspoiled countryside. You might also want to take part in a May Day rally, protesting against globalization and promoting better conditions for workers.

Whatever you do, get out there and shake the darkness off. The summer starts here. Hoooray!

## LowTide (the Saturday in May with the lowest tide – it depends on the moon)

If you only celebrate two festivals all year, LowTide should be one and Earth Day the other. Neither is a religious festival but the religious are invited to join in. LowTide events have been held around the coast of the UK, Ireland, Canada, America, Europe and Australia, celebrating one tide around one world because we all live downstream.

If you want to help organize a LowTide festival event or find out if one is being held near you, get in touch with riverOcean – their details are on page 236. This is because tidal areas are fraught with dangers for the unwary. The Goddess gives, but she can also bite.

RiverOcean can advise on safety and offer suggestions on what you might want to include. Events generally tend to be a marriage of arts and science. There might be story-telling, puppet shows, rock-pool talks, drumming workshops and surfing displays. There will also be oodles of environmental information and lots of (no)alternatives to make friends with. Basically it's a beach party with attitude.

## Summer Solstice (20/22 June)

The sun is at its greatest power around the summer solstice. Many pagans visit ancient sacred sites such as Avebury or Stonehenge. I prefer to party in my garden with members of our community. People from all walks of life are invited to trade ideas, business cards and contacts. We provide blankets, cushions and anything needed to make guests comfortable. Everyone must be warm. We light the garden with floating candles in jam jars which are strung from the trees and lined along paths.

We stay awake all night to welcome the dawn, the new phase in the wheel of the year. We look forward to the harvest and the changes that come with the roll towards winter and darkness. At dawn we bathe our faces in dew – the only "glamour spell" in my Book of Shadows. The most magically beautifying dew collects on the leaves of *Alchemilla mollis*, also known as ladies' mantle.

A coven member cooks elderflower fritters. The elder is the most sacred of witches' plants. It is never burned on fires. But the flowers may be eaten and the berries are great in the autumn for making compote, wine and cordial (go find a recipe book, my lovelies).

## Lughnasa (1 August or thereabouts)

A sabbat of bonfires and drums to celebrate the first harvest. It is a moveable feast since there's no point in giving thanks for a crop that has yet to be gathered .

Because our food comes from all around the world and we're emotionally engaged with one another as citizens of one earth, it's only polite to acknowledge what's happening in other places. If there is a drought and famine, in Africa, for example, or flooding and famine in Asia, it might be rather

# Elderflower fritters

**elderflowers with enough stalk attached
to make them easy to handle.
4 rounded teaspoons plain white flour
1 organic egg
300ml/½ pint milk
an eggcup full of water
a pan of oil**

Mix the batter. It shouldn't need to stand for too long, since you're using white flour which soaks up the liquid more quickly than wholemeal flour. If using brown flour, let the batter stand for half an hour and use a bit more milk and water.

The batter is the right consistency when the flower heads spring back into shape after being dipped, rather than hanging down looking gloopy and heavy under the weight of the batter.

Heat the oil. When the temperature is high, dip a flower head into the batter and allow the excess to drip back in to the bowl. Place the elderflower in the oil and cook until golden brown.

Serve in a lined wicker basket, accompanied by elderberrry compote made the year before. Alternatively smash strawberries and mix with chopped mint.

tasteless to party like there's no tomorrow because "we're all right, Jack".

Cast spells, offer libations for the people dealing with the effects of global warming, the ravages of war and the downsides of intensive farming head on. Bang your drums loudly so that their Gods might hear as well as Lugh, the

Irish God of light, to whom Lughnasa is dedicated.

This is a time for making sacrifices. Dig deep into your allowance and send money to an aid charity. It's a mermaid's teardrop in the ocean, but it is better than nothing at all.

Serve Irish soda bread, cheese, seasonal fruits. For the more globally minded, barbecue whole sweetcorn (maize) in their husks, eat rice and lentil salad and humous.

### Halloween (31 October)

We light candles and a fire, dress up and scare the kids senseless with ghost stories. Our coven provides trick or treaters with fruit and the chance to meet real witches! Serve pumpkin soup with roasted seeds and homemade bread.

### Yule (21 December)

Trees (real in a pot or fake) are decorated, fires and candles lit, scrummy roasted vegetables served and small gifts given. We celebrate the wheel turning – just six months to go until midsummer. This is the longest night of the year, a time when the landscape is barren. But it is also the time of rebirth, of light.

Plant garlic outdoors to be harvested at summer solstice.

### Christmas (25 December)

Pagans with children often celebrate Christmas. Packaging is kept to a minimum. (In the UK five times more rubbish is produced over the Christmas season than at any other time of year.) We make enquiries in the community and anyone who is to be alone is invited to join us.

Christians celebrate the story of the Nativity, the birth of Christ, of hope and of light. In more recent times Christmas became known as the season for over-indulgence and family rows. The Puritans banned it for this very reason, but it's back by popular demand.

The earth is our mother and we are all her children

ancient Hindu saying

# List of Deities

Here are a few outstanding immortal personalities for you to consider. Deities were so much more interesting in the old days, don't you think?

**Aphrodite** Greek Goddess, associated with the Roman Venus. She is a Goddess of love, war and victory, which means she's good to call on in matters of unrequited love or difficult relationships, where she can ensure all is fair. Aphrodite was born from the foam of the ocean following an unfortunate incident for her father. He was castrated and his genitals thrown into the sea, where by some feat of cosmic biology he sired a daughter.

**Artemis** winged Asian Mother Goddess who is always surrounded by animals. She presides over these wild creatures and helps girls when they start their periods and later when they give birth. The Greeks reinvented her as a virgin and many believe she has lived on disguised as the Virgin Mary. She is also seen as a moon Goddess and was known as Diana by the Romans.

**Cerridwen** Celtic Goddess of inspiration and poetry. She's a wise old woman who brewed a magic potion containing all the knowledge and wisdom of the past, present and future. This brew was accidentally drunk by her slave boy who went on to chronicle the adventures of King Arthur while entertaining and advising him at court as his bard.

**Cernunnos** Celtic fertility God depicted wearing antlers, a symbol of virility. He is associated with snakes, which are symbols of rejuvenation. He was never invited to join the Christian pantheon of saints, but he managed to stay visible, disguised as a green man with vegetation sprouting out of his mouth, on church buildings.

> # Love the world as yourself, then you can care for all things.
>
> ## Lao Tzu, Tao Te Ching

**Chantico** Aztec Goddess of the hearth, the heart of our homes. She reminds us that wood from carefully managed sources is the most sustainable form of heating known to the planet. Ash from the fire helps trees to grow.

**Dagda** Celtic good God, father of the tribe. By good, read practical rather than pious. He had a huge club and a cauldron with an inexhaustible supply of porridge, and he impregnated various fertility Goddesses to ensure good harvests.

**Epona** Celtic vegetation Goddess often depicted as a horse – a cool, unpolluting way to travel. White horses carved into hillsides in the south of England are said to be tributes to her because she accompanied the Celts on their journey to the Underworld in death. She is a popular Goddess with (no)alternatives since she represents the landscape, death and regeneration. Her return is a sign that it is time for action, with hope and rebirth rising from the land.

**Erzulie** Voodoo Goddess – of shopping. She is depicted as a beautiful wealthy young lady dripping with gold jewellery. Her sacred day is Friday, her sacred colour pink and her favourite drink champagne. Go there, girl.

**Estsanatlehi** Navajo fertility Goddess, the most powerful in their pantheon. She has the power of endless rejuvenation. She is the woman who changes. If she were ever canonized, she could become the patron saint of sustainability. In the summer she sends gentle rain and in spring thaws the snow.

**Lugh** Celtic sun God, celebrated at harvest time. He constantly got into scrapes with other Gods but, being well versed in the arts and warfare, instead of starting or continuing wars, he preferred to end them. He symbolizes the triumph of light over darkness.

**Men** Turkish moon God, ruler of our world and the underworld. He was invoked for healing.

**Ops** Roman Goddess of harvest and fertility. She may be invoked when seeds are planted. If canonization were offered she'd probably ask for the job of patron saint of non-genetically modified seeds, since she is said to regulate their growth

**Oshun** river Goddess from the Afro-Cuban religion Santeria. She casts love spells using pumpkins and is good for easing women's troubles.

**Sarasvati** Hindu mother Goddess and Goddess of wisdom. Her name means 'flowing waters'. She is inexhaustible in her powers since they derive from primeval waters. When offered gifts of pencils and pens she helps schoolchildren with their work. So place these offerings on your altar before exams.

**Yhi** Aboriginal sun Goddess, responsible for the creation of humankind. When she first opened her eyes, having been asleep in the primordial dreamtime, light fell upon the earth. As she walked, plants grew in her footsteps. Animals and then humans evolved from this environment. Yhi represents an uncannily accurate account of proceedings.

# Glossary

**Agenda 21** In 1992 leaders from every nation met at the Rio Conference on Environment and Development. All agreed that something had to be done to tackle environmental and social issues such as poverty. The strategy they all agreed upon was called Agenda 21. A decade later, hardly anyone has heard of it. But your local council may well employ a Local Agenda 21 officer. Write or phone to find out. Their job is to encourage communities to develop sustainable policies. These could be anything from tree-planting schemes to walking bus projects (organized walking to school in groups) and kerbside recycling.

Agenda 21 employees tend to be big on talk and lacking in funds. But if a community has the energy and will, *Yichallal!* It is possible and it can be done.

**Besom** broomstick. Symbolizes air, flying, freedom, spiritual purity. Excellent tool for sweeping floors.

**Climate change** unseasonal variations in weather patterns that see some areas inundated with rain while others experience drought conditions, an increase in tornadoes for some places and unusually warm winters in others. Climate change is caused by global warming.

**Drop-in coven** a loose collective of witches, pagans and sympathizers. Spells are cast, free of charge, for anyone who asks. The number one objective of the coven is to improve and increase awareness of the difficulties facing the world due to lack of respect for the Elements and for the needs of future generations. There is no high priestess or leader at a drop-in coven.

**Eco-footprint** this term describes the effects of our actions of the environment. (No)alternatives try to leave the minimum footprint, while others leave a ruddy great trail of destruction in their wake.

**Esbat** a meeting of witches on a full moon. A time for spells, rituals and contemplation.

**Global warming** a rise in the world's temperature due to an accumulation of greenhouse gases such as $CO_2$ in the atmosphere. These are generated through the burning of fossil fuels – in industry and transport. The destruction of rainforests adds to the problem because the trees would absorb some of these emissions. Global warming is melting glaciers and polar icecaps, causing the sea level to rise, consequently wiping many islands and eventually whole states and countries off the map. It is also responsible for climate change.

**(No)alternatives** people who believe the only way forward for humanity is to live within our means. Rather than ravaging the earth for the here and now – plus a quick profit – (no)alternatives believe resources should be preserved for future generations. Hence the motto: "Be a good ancestor."

**Sustainability** replacing what we use and conserving what we have. Think of our resources as money in a bank. Due to human activities we're currently running on overdraft. If we don't start saving, our world will soon be

bankrupt and it would take a mighty powerful God or Goddess to bail us out. The world might well recover in time, but we will be long gone, because without healthy Air, Water, Earth and the sensible use of Fire, life as we know it is unsustainable.

**TV** a 20th-century invention that controls thought and behaviour. Regular viewing encourages consumerism and prevents victims from engaging in constructive activities such as socializing, cooking and saving the world.

**Wiccan Rede** also known as the *Rede of the Wiccae*, this is a set of "commandments" written in poetry, outlining a moral blueprint for witches. Quotes from the *Wiccan Rede* that appear in this book are from this poem first published in *Green Egg Magazine*, Vol VIII No 69 (Ostara 1975). Attributed to Adriana Porter, it was brought to light by her granddaughter, Lady Gwen Thompson. The poem in its entirety can be read in Pete Jennings' book *Pagan Paths* (see page 231) or on most witchy websites. There are now more versions of the *Rede* than there are ways of stirring a cauldron.

See my works, how lovely they are, how fine they are. Take care not to corrupt and destroy my universe, for if you destroy it no one will come after you to put it right.

Genesis, The Bible

# Essential reading

The following books and authors have made me the person I am today: better than I was before reading them. I think you may find them helpful, too. Some inspire and all educate. Some are out of print – scour secondhand bookshops or look out for other books on similar topics.

## Spiritual matters

*Celtic Wisdom*, Vivianne Crowley, Thorsons, 1998
*Dictionary of Folklore*, David Pickering, Cassell, 1999
*Living Ancient Wisdom*, Paul Devereux, Rider, 2002
*Pagan Paths*, Pete Jennings, Rider, 2002
*Sacred Journey*, Sally Griffyn, Kyle Cathie, 2000

## Herbs and potions

*The Art of Aromatherapy*, Robert Tisserand, C W Daniel Company, 1996
*The Encyclopedia of Herbs and Herbalism*, ed Malcolm Stuart, Orbis, 1979
*The Handmade Soap Book*, Melinda Coss, New Holland,1998
*Herbal Celebrations Cookbook*, Noel Richardson and Jenny Cameron, Whitecap Books, 2000
*100 Great Natural Remedies*, Penelope Ody, Kyle Cathie, 1998
*A Modern Herbal* Mrs M Grieve FRHS, Tiger Books, 1994

## For green fingers

*Bob Flowerdew's Organic Bible*, Kyle Cathie, 1998
*Jekka's Complete Herb Book*, Kyle Cathie, 1997
*New Gardening for Wildlife*, Bill Merilees, Whitecap Books, 2000
*The New Indoor Plant Book*, John Evans, Kyle Cathie, 1993
*Urban Eden*, Adam and James Caplin, Kyle Cathie, 2000
*The Wildlife Garden Month-by-Month*, Jackie Bennet, David & Charles Books, 1993

## Cookery

*The Cranks Recipe Book*, David and Kay Canter and Daphne Swann, Grafton Books, 1990
*Vegetarian Comfort Food*, Jennifer Warren, Whitecap Books, 2001
*Vegetarian Kitchen*, Sarah Brown, BBC, 1984

## Eco stuff

*Blueprint for a Green Planet*, John Seymour and Herbert Girard, Dorling Kindersley, 1987
*Earth and Faith: a book of reflection for action*, UNEP. Order from **www.earthprint.com**
*Generation FIX*, Beyond Words, 2002
*Go Mad! 365 Daily Ways to Save the Planet*, The Ecologist, 2001
*The Good Seed Guide: all you need to know about planting trees from seed*, The Tree Council, 51 Catherine Place, London SW1 6DY or **www.treecouncil.org.uk**
*Save or Delete, a last chance to save the world's ancient forests*, Greenpeace

## Cool Reads

*Alice in Wonderland* and *Through the Looking Glass*, Lewis Carroll (written well over a hundred years ago, but still magical)
*Canadian Girls Who Rocked the World*, Tanya Lloyd, Whitecap Books, 2001
*Go Ask Alice*, anonymous true story of a teenage drug addict, Eyre Methuen, 1972, available in paperback from Arrow Books
*Harry Potter* series by J.K. Rowling, Bloomsbury (UK), Scholastic (US)

*In Quest of a Remedy*, Shiram Jaiswal, edited by Pat Bowen, riverOcean, 2001 – order through **www.rore.org.uk**

*Lord of the Rings*, J R R Tolkien, Allen & Unwin, 1954-5; in paperback from HarperCollins

*The Sorceress*, Celia Rees, Bloomsbury (UK), Candlewick Press (US), 2002

*Sweep* series by Cate Tiernan, Puffin

*Witch Child*, Celia Rees, Bloomsbury (UK), Candlewick Press (US), 2000

Today we understand that the future of humanity very much depends on our planet and that the future of the planet very much depends on humanity.

His Holiness The Dalai Lama of Tibet

# Useful Addresses

## World-saving organizations and companies

All UK sites listed either have links to other countries, provide information that applies worldwide or can deliver to anywhere in the world.

### Actionaid
**www.actionaid.org**
Fighting to end poverty, ban GM foods and promote fairtrade links whereby farmers and others receive a fair price for their goods.

### Amnesty International
**www.amnesty.org.uk**
Highlights the plight of torture victims and those who are imprisoned for speaking out against undemocratic regimes.

### Befrienders International
**www.befrienders.org**
A volunteer-based organization helping to prevent suicide in over 40 countries.

### Campaign for Nuclear Disarmament
**www.cnduk.org**
or **youthstudentcnd.org.uk**
A favourite with activist grannies, the organization has a youth branch and can tell you when the rallies are. They also produce *Now* magazine, which is worth a look.

### Campaign for Real Events
**www.c-realevents.demon.co.uk**
Can advise on DIY cycle generators – creating energy to run a PA via pedal power.

### Care2
**www.care2.com**
This is an environmental network with lots of great information on healthy living and a healthy planet.

### Centre for Alternative Technology
**www.cat.org.uk**
Promotes sustainable methods for everything from building techniques to food production. Great kids section.

### Center for Great Lakes Environmental Education
**www.greatlakesed.org**
Great links for youth and teachers that emphasize the environmental challenges facing these immense lakes.

### David Suzuki Foundation
**www.davidsuzuki.org**
Canadian foundation searching to find a balance between social, economic and ecological needs.

### Druids
**www.warband.org**
Excellent druid sight from King Arthur Uther Pendragon, a dedicated eco-warrior who has done much to change peoples' attitudes to road developments and shown the conservation of sacred sites in a whole new light.

### E Magazine
**www.emagazine.com**
An environmental magazine with a great website.

### Earth Day Network
**www.earthday.net**
Start here if you want to organize an Earth Day event in April. It offers everything from ideas to links with organizations all around the world that are involved in this growing movement.

### Ecos Paints
**www.ecospaints.com**
Unit 34, Heysham Business Park, Middleton Road, Heysham, LA3 3PP.
0044 (0)1524 852371
For chemical-free paints in lots of great colours. Sample pots are available.

## The Ecologist
www.theecologist.co.uk
Scary facts from the top environmental magazine's website.

## Freeplay
www.freeplay.net
Buy your Trevor Baylis-invented clockwork radio here. Plenty of styles to choose from.

## Friends of the Earth
www.foe.co.uk
An international network of right-on (no)alternatives. Provides back-up for demonstrations (legal advice for eco-warriors) and will also help you slim your bin. What a dedicated bunch.

## Greenpeace
www.greenpeace.org.uk
More militant than FOE, campaigners sometimes risk their lives to put the environment on the front pages of our newspapers. They do a lot of ground- and ball-breaking investigative work, too. So support them. Outside the UK, check out
www.greenpeace.org
and stay informed on their various global campaigns.

## Green Choices
www.greenchoices.org
Do the quiz to see how green you are. Then find out how to deepen your shade of green.

## Grist Magazine
www.gristmagazine.com
An online news service. Subscription is free and can provide you with daily, weekly or monthly bulletins on the latest eco news. It's written with humour but it still scares the pants off me.

## Healthy Interiors
www.healthyhomeinteriors.com
Our choice of building materials or furnishings should not have a negative impact on the environment. Buy everything from organic cotton sheets to sustainably harvested wood.

## The Hemp Shop
www.thehemp-shop.com
Sells everything from lip balm to clothing via food and shampoos. If it can be manufactured from hemp they'll sell it and deliver anywhere in the world.

## Hostelling International
www.iyhf.org
Information on hostelling, travelling and budgeting your way around the world.

## IFAW charitable trust
www.ifaw.org
Acts to improve animal welfare, by preserving habitat and reducing commercial exploitation of animals.

## International Tree Foundation
www.tree-foundation.org.uk
Explains the importance of trees and how thoughtful tree-planting can save whole villages in vulnerable parts of the world. A worthwhile charity indeed. They have a beautiful motto: *Twahamwe*, which is Swahili for "All as one".

## LETS Scheme
www.letslink.co.uk
All you need to know about trading in favours rather than cash.

## Mooncup
www.mooncup.co.uk
Find out about the most eco-friendly of sanitary protection. You can buy online too, or check out your local health-food store.

**PeTA**
**www.peta.org**
Anti-fur campaigners who believe animals are not ours to eat, wear, experiment on or use for entertainment.

**Planet Ark**
**www.planetark.org**
A round-up of environmental news – not as funny as Grist, but extremely moving at times.

**Positive Power**
**www.positivepower.co.uk**
Lots of info on renewable sources of energy from a company that organizes solar-powered raves.

**Radical Routes**
**www.radicalroutes.org.uk**
A co-operative linking a network of small groups and individuals working for a sustainable present and future. Can advise on anything from LETS schemes to tree planting and veg-box distribution.

**Rising Tide**
**www.risingtide.org.uk**
Offers advice, training and support on how to run local campaigns against climate change.

**riverOcean**
**www.riverocean.org.uk**
For details of LowTide festivals, to order lunar calendars and a fantastic set of links. The research for this book began at this site.

**Sierra Club**
**www.sierraclub.org**
Learn more about this highly successful grassroots advocacy organization.

**Soil Association**
**www.soilassociation.org**
Promotes organic food and farming. Can tell you where your nearest supplier is, plus loads of other useful info.

**Spirit of Nature**
**www.spiritofnature.co.uk**
Green products, including sanitary protection that can be delivered anywhere in the world.

**Starhawk**
**www.starhawk.org**
Find out about globalization from the world's leading eco-witch. Starhawk is a wise woman who leads by example. Let her be an inspiration to us all.

**Sustrans**
**www.sustrans.org.uk**
They design and build traffic-free routes for cyclists, walkers and people with disabilities. A good start for anyone planning to get on their bike and sort the car problem.

**TakingITGlobal**
**www.takingitglobal.com**
Devoted to encouraging young people to believe in themselves, and to fostering leadership and social entrepreneurship through the innovative use of technology.

**Time Dollars**
**www.timedollar.org**
American version of LETS scheme, whereby communities are bonded through working together, trading favours rather than cash.

**Tourism Concern**
**www.tourismconcern.org.uk**
How green is your holiday destination? This group explores the impact of tourism on communities.

**The Tree Council**
**www.treecouncil.org.uk**
Everything you need to know about planting trees from seed or saplings. They produce a good booklet explaining how, too. See essential reading, page 231.

**Tree Spirit**
Hawkbatch Farm
Arley
Bewdley
Worcestershire
DY12 2AH
A voluntary group planting and growing trees for our future.

**UK Rivers**
**www.ukrivers.net**
Loads of info and links explaining the importance of rivers – great starting point for homework and school projects.

**Unit[e]**
**www.unit-e.co.uk**
A home energy supplier using only sustainable sources such as wind and willow. Ask your parents to sign up today.

**United Nations Environment Programme**
**www.unep.org**
An organization which understands that faith plays an integral part in redefining humanity's relationship with its environment. Praying – to whichever God or Goddess suits you – has never been so cool. They also have loads of eco-info.

**Vegetarian Society**
**www.vegsoc.org**
Recipes, info and advice on becoming a vegetarian. There's a special section for teenagers.

**Wiggly Wigglers**
**www.wigglywigglers.co.uk**
Innovative mail order company specializing in accessories for wildlife gardens. Also sells wormeries and water butts made from recycled plastic.

**Woodcraft Folk**
**www.woodcraftfolk.org.uk**
A UK-based organization with international links, Woodcraft Folk is a (no)alternative to Scouts, Cubs, Guides and other groups with a militaristic approach to the great outdoors. The site has excellent eco info for young people and is an organization well worth joining.

**Women's Environmental Network**
**www.wen.org.uk**
Includes info on sanitary protection, GM food and toxic chemicals from the female perspective.

**Worldwide Fund for nature**
**www.wwf-uk.org**
Excellent starting point if you want to save the whale or a panda. Outside the UK, go for
**www.wwf.org**
Help to stop the degradation of the planet's natural environment and build a future in which humans live in harmony with nature using this site's great resources.

**Worldwide Workers on Organic Farms**
**www.wwoof.org**
Want to work on an organic farm? This site provides details of where and how to apply, worldwide.

**OTHER STUFF**
Here's just a few sites that I've found useful. You might, too.

**Alcohol Concern**
**www.alcoholconcern.org.uk**
Advises on drinking safely and stopping altogether.

**Blossom Candles**
PO Box 468, Haywards Heath, West Sussex, RH16 2YF
01444 487 719
The best undyed pure beeswax candles in the world.

**British Union Against Vivisection**
**www.buav.org**
BUAV can tell you all about beauty products that haven't been tested on animals.

**Campaign for Tobacco Free Kids**
**www.tobaccofreekids.com**
Interesting stuff about how tobacco companies exploit you and workers in the developing world. This site is not square at all. On a shoestring budget a group of Americans are taking on this multi-billion-dollar industry. Even chain smokers should back them.

**Childline**
**www.childline.org.uk**
Helpline number: 0800 1111
Freepost 1111 London N1 0BR
Help at the end of a telephone for UK dialers with problems ranging from abuse to bereavement and racism. For overseas enquiries visit the website

**Comfort and Joy**
**www.comfortandjoy.co.uk**
Top-quality beauty products (skincare, cosmetics, shampoos) made fresh to order with organic herbs and wildcrafted essential oils (it means the plants are found growing wild or grown on small farms rather than plantations). Honeymoon cleanser and Clued Up cleansing scrub are cult hits among teenage witches the world over.

**Fossil2000**
**www.fossil2000.co.uk**
For crystals, crystal balls and geodes. It's best to select your own but if you can't the shopkeepers at Fossil 2000 will choose in a sympathetic manner for you.

They also sell DeoKrystal. Made from a crystal called alunite, you rub it on your armpits for a hundred per cent natural deodorant.

**Joseph Institute of Ethics**
**www.josephsoninstitute.org**
Lots of valuable info on being a good person with sound ethics.

**Minor Arcana.**
**www.minorarcana.org.co.uk**
Advice, magazines and general support for teen witches, brought to you by the youth branch of the Pagan Federation, who can be found at
**www.paganfed.org**

**Release**
**www.release.org.uk**
Impartial drug advice, information and support for users and their families.

**Relate**
**relate.org.uk**
Advises on family relationships and helps you cope with your parents' divorce

**Samaritans**
**www.samaritans.org.uk**
0345 90 90 90
A listening ear, day and night, when you can't cope with your life, for whatever reason. Outside the UK, send an email and you will receive a reply.

**Wiccan Rede Project**
**www.pagan.drak.net/sheathomas/**
Offers a fascinating insight into the history and meaning of the *Wiccan Rede*. The best site of its kind on the web.

**Young Minds**
**www.youngminds.org.uk**
For advice on everything from eating disorders to self-injury.

**Youth Hostel Association**
**www.yha.org.uk**
Information on hostels worldwide, providing cheap accommodation for travellers.

# Index